IT, DREAM IT, WRITE
GROW IT, DREAM IT
IT, GROW IT, DREAM
SHARE IT, GROW IT, DREAM IT, WRITE
T, SHARE IT, GROW IT, DREAM IT, WR
MAKE IT, SHARE IT, GROW IT, DREAM
T, MAKE IT, SHARE IT, GROW IT, DREA
CAST IT, MAKE IT, SHARE IT, GROW I
IT, CAST IT, MAKE IT, SHARE IT, GRO
T, HOST IT, CAST IT, MAKE IT, SHARE
E IT, HOST IT, CAST IT, MAKE IT, SHA
, WRITE IT, HOST IT, CAST IT, MAKE
M IT, WRITE IT, HOST IT, CAST IT, MA
, DREAM IT, WRITE IT, HOST IT, CAST
IT, DREAM IT, WRITE IT, HOST IT, CA
GROW IT, DREAM IT, WRITE IT, HOST
IT, GROW IT, DREAM IT, WRITE IT, H
SHARE IT, GROW IT, DREAM IT, WRITE
T, SHARE IT, GROW IT, DREAM IT, WR

SO YOU WANT TO
START A PODCAST

SO YOU WANT TO
START A PODCAST

Finding Your Voice, Telling Your Story, and
Building a Community That Will Listen

KRISTEN MEINZER

WM

WILLIAM MORROW

An Imprint of HarperCollins *Publishers*

HarperCollins books may be purchased for educational, business, or sales promotional use. For information, please email the Special Markets Department at SPsales@harpercollins.com.

FIRST EDITION

Library of Congress Cataloging-in-Publication Data has been applied for.

ISBN 978-0-06-293667-7

19 20 21 22 23 LSC 10 9 8 7 6 5 4 3 2 1

FOR DEAN.

You are so good at everything you do, and being with you
makes me better at everything I do.

Contents

Part 3 HOST IT

Part 4 CAST IT

Part 5 MAKE IT

Part 6 SHARE IT

Part 7 GROW IT

Introduction

Hello, you magnificent creature. Yes, you, who just opened this book. I want to tell you something, something that you deserve to hear but perhaps don't hear enough: I believe in you. I believe you have great stories in you that people want to hear. I believe you are something special. Don't ever let anyone tell you otherwise.

The question, of course, is not whether you're magnificent (you are) but whether you want to translate your magnificence into a podcast. And that's reason number one why I'm here: to help you figure that out. Reason number two: to help you make your podcast a reality, if podcasting is what your heart truly desires.

Now, you might be saying at this point: "Of course I want to start a podcast! That's why I picked up this book! Why are you even questioning my intentions?"

Here's why, gentle readers: because podcasting can be hard. It can be confusing. It can leave you wondering why you ever thought it would be a good idea. I want you to know not only about the joys that lie ahead, but also about the work that will be required to make those joys materialize. I want you to do better than I did starting out. I want you to know that I and others are a resource for you.

Warning: I'm going to ask you some tough questions: questions that every podcaster should, to my mind, ask themselves in order to do the best job they can. These questions will involve some soul searching. And I'm going to expect you to do some serious work.

And regardless of whether you end up creating the next Serial at the end of all this, or making a tiny little show for just your family and closest friends, I want you to remember: You're magnificent.

Why Me? (a.k.a. What Qualifies This Person to Give Advice?)

You might be asking: Who is this person who's simultaneously telling me I'm magnificent and sending me warnings? What does she know about me, and, more important, what does she know about podcasting?

First and foremost, I'm a podcast host. I've hosted three successful podcasts in the past ten years, the audiences of which exceed ten million. The first show, Movie Date, was a production of WNYC (the same folks behind Radiolab and Death, Sex, and Money), and ran for six years. The show had a fairly modest following but a very notable guest list, including Scarlett Johansson, Joan Rivers, Christina Hendricks, James Franco, Clive Owen, Taraji P. Henson, and loads of other famous and respected actors, directors, and writers. Each week, my beloved co-host Rafer Guzman and I would interview stars, review new movies, quiz listeners with movie trivia, and dispense what we called Movie Therapy (listeners would write and call in with their life issues, and we would give them a prescription of movies to watch to help them through their predicaments).

My next two hosting gigs were with Panoply (the powerhouse behind Revisionist History, You Must Remember This, and Happier with Gretchen Rubin).

One show, When Meghan Met Harry: A Royal Weddingcast, was fairly short lived by design. As the title suggests, it was a countdown to the royal nuptials of Prince Harry and Meghan Markle, and it was nothing short of a six-month obsessive lovefest. Each week, my pal James Barr and I discussed the latest headlines, interviewed experts, provided explainers on various bits of royal protocol, and made predictions for the big day itself. The show garnered international attention, landing us on the BBC, CBC, TLC, and NBC, among several other networks. It was named a top fifty podcast by *Time* and a top forty podcast by *Cosmopolitan* and was showcased in dozens of other press outlets. The show was even featured on British Airways flights for the month of May 2018.

And then there is the show I love and continue to host with my dear friend Jolenta Greenberg: By the Book. Part reality show, part self-help podcast, By the Book has, in my opinion, changed what a podcast can be, and is currently wrapping up its fifth season. In each episode of the show, Jolenta and I choose a different self-help book to live by, follow it to the letter for two weeks, and weigh in on whether the book was actually life changing. Along the way, we eat what each book tells us to eat, we dress as we're told to dress, we change our sleeping patterns and vocabulary and even our sex lives. And as with any reality show you'd see on TV, we record ourselves throughout—at home, at work, with our husbands and friends, at our best and at our very worst. By the Book repeatedly lands on "best of" lists—it's been named a top nine podcast by NPR, named a top twenty-one podcast by BuzzFeed, was picked as a *New York Times* Podcast Club pick—and it's covered in the media almost every week.

While hosting might be what I'm best known for, I'm also a podcast producer. I've produced live, daily, national news shows. I've produced podcasts about food and entrepreneurship and music and parenting and mental health. I've worked on award-winning shows with famous hosts and produced podcasts for notable brands, and I've even helped produce audio projects with small children. The shows I've produced include Happier with Gretchen Rubin, Happier in Hollywood, Girlboss Radio, The Sporkful, Food52's Burnt Toast, Spawned with Kristen and Liz, Side Hustle School, Quiet: The Power of Introverts with Susan Cain, *Vanity Fair*'s Little Gold Men, Soundcheck, Inc. Uncensored, and the *Real Simple* Podcasts, to name a few.

With a number of these shows, I was doing far more than just scriptwriting, booking guests, engineering, coaching hosts, and cutting tape—I was also doing show development: creating the concept or shape of the show from day one. Show development is something I also did for CBS TV before my audio days, and it's something I continue to do for clients on a contract basis.

Outside the studio, I've taught classes on audio production at such respected institutions as Columbia University, Brooklyn College, the Craig Newmark Graduate School of Journalism at CUNY, and Hunter College. I've been a regular presenter at the Brooklyn Historical Society, discussing history and pop culture. I've appeared as a commentator on the BBC, CBC, Vox, Australian Broadcasting Corp., Radio New Zealand, multiple *Slate* podcasts, multiple WNYC programs, and dozens of other shows and outlets, large and small. And I speak on average once a month at conferences (recent conventions include the BlogHer Creators Summit, Podcast Movement, the IAB Podcast Upfront, Werk It, and the On Air Fest), where attendance ranges from a few hundred to many thousands.

Between all my media and conference appearances, many millions of people have heard and seen me speak. Each week, more than fourteen million people listen to All Things Considered, a show I've appeared on more than once. Two million people listened to me on WNYC every Friday for six years when I was a regular on-air contributor. Millions of people watched the three hour-long TLC royal wedding documentaries in which I appeared in May 2018. And millions of Gretchen Rubin fans know me as her former producer and occasional guest.

I'm qualified. And more important: I'm here to help.

What This Book Is, What This Book Isn't

Friends, I sincerely hope that this book will be more to you than just a podcasting guidebook. My dream is that it will be the motivation you need to find your voice, the confirmation that your story matters, and the cheering squad you wish for when you're feeling most discouraged.

But beyond the instruction and encouragement and love, this book is also about the tough stuff: ideation, direction, structure, storytelling, soul-searching, and all the other elements that are central to making a great podcast. I'm talking art. I'm talking heart. I'm talking craft. I'm talking about the stuff that most handbooks and blog entries and listicles don't cover.

To put it bluntly, I want this book to fill you with both information and affirmation. I want it to be a toolbox you can both rely on and stand on as you share what's in your heart. It's the least you deserve.

Now that that's out of the way, I must also tell you what this book isn't: a technical guide. And by that I mean:

* I'm not going to compare and contrast all the latest and greatest podcasting gizmos and gadgets in this book. Yes, I'll tell you the basics of what equipment I consider necessary (it's a lot less stuff than you might imagine), but I won't be advocating for specific name brands or listing off the benefits of this line of products versus that one.

* I'm not going to explain how to use all the equipment or software out there. In my opinion, it's far better to learn

how to use studio equipment and editing software from a person—either on the job, at a workshop, in a classroom, from a private tutor, or at a meet-up. Second to that, I recommend video tutorials. That's because the job of recording and editing involves so many senses. When you do it, your ears are filled with a variety of sounds as your eyes take in multiple moving tracks and your fingers hit shortcuts on your keyboard and adjust levels with your mouse. And with each brand of software and piece of equipment, your ears, eyes, and hands will be used in totally different ways. More than once, I've tried to teach myself how to use various kinds of editing software—only to fail miserably. In the end, it was only with the help of patient and supportive colleagues that I reached a point of mastery. Give yourself the same gift I did: the help of humans.

All that being said, my honest belief is that learning to use gadgets is the easy part. The hard part is everything else: figuring out why you and the world need your show, telling your story in a way that's authentic to you, and making sure your message is delivered in a beautiful and compelling way.

Are you ready? Of course you are.

Part 1

DREAM IT

Know Why You Want to Start a Podcast

When Jolenta Greenberg and I first pitched the idea of By the Book to Panoply, we had to bring our A game. This was the company that made shows for powerhouses like Malcolm Gladwell and Gretchen Rubin. We needed to prove we were worth investing in.

Fortunately, we knew we had a good idea: Two good friends—one a self-help believer and the other a skeptic—would live by self-help books for two weeks at a time. While we lived by the books, we'd also record ourselves at work, at home, and in the world, to show how the books made our lives better or worse. It would be a comedy show! It would be a reality show! It would be a book review podcast!

The folks we were pitching to were intrigued. But they also had one big question: "Why?" Or, more specifically: "Why do you want to start a podcast?"

This may seem like the simplest question in the world. Or perhaps it may seem like the hardest. Either way, it's the most important question to ask yourself as you embark on this journey, and it's the first question I ask every person who's ever told me they want to start their own show—whether that person is a best-selling author or a college student.

Here's the number one reason people give me: "Because everyone is doing it."

And here's my gut reaction when I hear that answer: *That's not a good enough reason.*

This isn't to say that I haven't also done things because everyone else was. I have, in big and small ways. I put up with lousy boyfriends, I wore horrible clothes that looked terrible on my figure, I pretended to like British comedy.

(Note on British comedy: If you love it, I wish you thousands more hours of watching and laughing. But I hate cringing, and it so happens that cringing is half of what British comedy is, and why would I put up with years of sitting through something I don't enjoy? Oh yeah, because everyone around me was.)

This leads back to my point: "Everyone is doing it" is *not* a good reason. This is why parents for millions of years have said to their kids, "If everyone else jumped off a bridge, would you do it too?" At which point, kids throughout history, dazzled by their peers, have answered, "Duh, no," right before jumping off a bridge.

You need to have a better reason to start a podcast than "everyone is doing it."

When pitching By the Book to Panoply, these are the reasons Jolenta and I gave:

* We wanted to push the boundaries of what a podcast could sound like. At the time, almost every show seemed to be drawing its inspiration from public radio, or in some cases talk radio. We were drawing our inspiration from reality TV.

* We wanted to relay empowering, intersectional feminist messages to our listeners in a format that felt like pure en-

tertainment rather than broccoli. Again, at the time, this was rare. Most shows tended to feature straightforward discussions (or monologues or lectures) on ideology.

Of course, there are hundreds of right answers to this question. Here are just a few brief reasons I've heard other podcasters give:

- I want to build community around an issue or identity.
- I want to spread the word about something I'm very passionate about.
- I have a specific skill (foreign language proficiency, business knowledge, and so on) that I'd like to teach.
- I am an entrepreneur who sees a podcast as one additional way to grow my brand.
- I want to give my readers/viewers/customers an additional way to access my content.

Now, think about your "why." No doubt, you have lots of good reasons beyond "everyone is doing it."

But hopefully, your reasons don't include the second-most-common answer I hear from aspiring podcasters: "My friend Dave and I are really funny."

To expand on this a bit: "Dave and I can literally talk about anything and crack each other up for hours. It doesn't matter the subject."

You know what? I believe you when you say Dave is funny. I'm sure he makes you laugh every time you see him. And I'm sure you're also very witty. You have a glint in your eye that tells me you make keen observations that are both self-effacing and truly charming. I like you!

But let's dig a little deeper into this: Without any context, am I going to get your jokes? And is the humor you and Dave share enough of a reason to start a podcast?

I'm going to posit my opinion here: no.

This isn't to say that you and Dave shouldn't start a podcast. You and Dave may very well have it in you to start the best, funniest podcast that will ever exist. But you need to think hard about a solid reason you and Dave should start your show.

Here are a few examples other funny people have come up with for starting a podcast:

* We found a porno novel my dad wrote a long time ago and want to dissect it chapter by chapter.
* We want to dive into the history of bad movies in a way that no college class would.
* We think that current events can be depressing and we know we can put a fun spin on them.
* We love true crime but prefer to laugh about it rather than cry about it.

I hope I haven't discouraged you and Dave. Rather, I hope I've inspired you to start thinking more concretely about why you want a show. Hopefully, you're jotting down ideas and fist-pumping the air and feeling amped and ready for the next chapter and the next chapter after that.

But before we get to those chapters, let's hit on one final point about why you want to start a podcast.

Reminder: The first way I asked the question put the emphasis on the "why." *Why* do you want to start a podcast?

But now I'm going to put the emphasis on the "podcast." Why do you want to start a *podcast*?

Specifically, I want you to think about why you want to start a podcast versus a blog, book, YouTube channel, Pinterest board, Instagram feed, and so on. Is a podcast really the best way to tell your story? Is your story so visual that a podcast will fail to do it justice? Will your story be more effective if it's written out, or told as a stand-up comedy routine, or shaped into a multimedia interactive sculpture?

Don't undersell your great idea by wedging it into a podcast.

In short: Even if you have a good reason to start a podcast, is a podcast really the best way to showcase your magnificence?

If it is, keep reading.

2

Recognize Who Your Show Is For

Your voice is a gift. Your story is a gift. Your knowledge, sense of humor, insights, experiences: They're all gifts.

The big question: Who do you want to give those gifts to?

Or, to put it more bluntly: Who is your podcast for?

Keep in mind that it's for somebody. If it wasn't, you wouldn't be recording it and releasing it into the world.

Take a moment right now and imagine the person who would listen to your podcast. Where does she live? What kind of family unit is he a part of? What is a typical day in your listener's life like? What does she agonize about? What does he do for fun?

This is an exercise I was taught by my friend and former colleague Andrea Silenzi, who hosts the hugely popular podcasts Why Oh Why and The Longest Shortest Time. When Andrea imagined a Why Oh Why listener, she thought of a person we both know in real life named Jenny. Jenny now has a boyfriend, but up until recently she was unattached. Jenny loves her job but doesn't feel married to it. Jenny is funny and self-effacing. Jenny lives in an urban area and is under thirty-five.

Andrea said that anytime she felt unsure about anything she was doing with her show, she'd imagine Jenny. How would Jenny feel about this? Would Jenny get the joke? Would Jenny feel affirmed by this?

I did the same exercise in the early days of By the Book. I imagined who would be listening. At the top of my list: two kind, funny best friends—one black and one white, one gay and one straight—named Louise and Anwar. Louise and Anwar don't always feel great about themselves, but they usually look on the bright side. Neither of them is married, but both believe in love. Each week, together they watch one of the reality shows they're addicted to while sipping wine or margaritas. Neither of them is what you would call a podcast super-listener, with thirty-plus shows in their queue. In fact, both Louise and Anwar started listening to podcasts only in the last year or two. Louise and Anwar are smart, well-read, and don't like being preached to. Neither of them sat at the cool table in high school, but neither did I, and they are absolutely the people I'd most want to spend time with now.

I love Louise and Anwar, even though they are imaginary. They're who I'm accountable to and who I want to entertain, and occasionally they're also the ones who let me off the hook when I need it.

For example, in the first season of By the Book, Jolenta and I heard from a number of angry folks who hated the fact that we swore. The letter writers would call us "ignorant-sounding" or claim that we were undermining our stories with our foul language. Some said they made it their mission to tell everyone they knew not to listen to our show because it was too offensive.

Initially, the letters had me worried. Should we change up the show? Was the explicit language warning at the top of each episode not enough? How would Jolenta and I sound like ourselves through the traumas we subjected ourselves to each week if we stopped using barnyard language?

This is where Louise and Anwar came to the rescue. I imagined sitting on the sofa with them and watching the *Property Brothers* while the two of them laughed about all those critical comments.

"I'd also swear if a book forced me to starve myself for forty-eight hours," Anwar would say, downing his prosecco.

"Fuck, I'm swearing like a sailor just thinking about it," Louise would reply, refilling Anwar's glass.

If Louise and Anwar were okay with what Jolenta and I were doing, then that was good enough for me.

Note: Just because Louise and Anwar are the listeners I think of when I'm in a By the Book pickle, it doesn't mean they're the only ones I care about. I care about all our listeners. But who are they?

Broadly speaking, they're the ones I say I'm targeting in official meetings and documents: self-help lovers, self-help haters, feminists, and comedy fans.

Less broadly speaking, they include: single mothers, men who listen with their wives, white women who are realizing their own racial biases, women of color who feel unseen by other podcast hosts, teenage misfits, retired misfits, insecure weirdos who are relieved to feel less alone in their insecurities, and people who long to feel lovable—especially to themselves.

I care about all of them and I try to speak to them, but I know I can't always make them happy with what I say into a microphone or how I say it. I can, however, think about Louise and Anwar.

Now, think about your own ideal listener. Think about who you'd want to spend time with, or who you want to reach. Think about them in at least as much detail as I think about Louise and Anwar.

Next: Think about why your imaginary listeners would choose to play your podcast versus turn on the radio, watch TV, or listen to another podcast. What are you giving them that others aren't?

In the case of By the Book, Jolenta and I figured we could give self-help lovers crib notes and self-help haters more fuel for their cocktail chatter. We hoped we'd give reality TV lovers a new way of consuming stunt stories. We dreamed we could fill a tiny bit of the hole left behind by Oprah. And we hoped we'd find a place in the world for listeners who want to start or end their days with a bit of laughter.

One thing we didn't plan on: For many listeners, we simply serve as good company. Some have written in to say we're the gals they eavesdrop on at the next table, supporting each other without any hints of underlying jealousy or competition. Others have said we're their virtual support group, because we're so open about our mistakes, flaws, insecurities, and accomplishments. And a few listeners have even told us that they consider us their imaginary friends—an admission that we accept as the highest of compliments.

One final thought to consider before moving on to the next chapter: It may be the case that your ideal listener is you and only you. In other words, your dream podcast may really be a dream audio diary. And if that's the case, that's 100 percent fine. After all, there are no ears more important in this adventure than your own.

Podcast Listeners by the Numbers

From the Edison Research Podcast Consumer study, 2018

- 70 percent of podcast listeners are between 18 and 54.

- They are almost equally male and female.

- Podcast listeners tend to have a higher level of educational attainment than non-listeners. 34 percent have some graduate education or a graduate degree versus 23 percent of non-listeners.

- 51 percent of podcast listeners earn between $75,000 and $150,000 per year.

3

Decide What Your Show Is About

I'm willing to bet that you have some idea of what your show is about. When I ask prospective podcasters, they usually do. But more often than not, the idea is not really a show idea. It's just a subject matter.

For example, a lot of people over the years have said to me, "I want to host a podcast about movies."

Now, let me make myself clear: I love movies. I spent hours in film studies classes in college. I used to co-host a podcast in which movies were central to the show. But "a show about movies" really isn't a show at all. Movies are just a topic.

Consider this: Which sounds more like an actual show idea to you:

* a podcast about movies
* a podcast in which a film critic interviews a real person each week who's lived the same experience as a character in a newly released film?

If you guessed that the second answer is the actual show idea, you are correct. In fact, it's the show idea that my friend Rafer Guzman first came up with in late 2009. At the time, I was working for a public radio show as the culture producer. Rafer, who's a film critic for *Newsday*, was one of the contributors I worked closely with.

But Rafer didn't just want to be a contributor on the radio. "I want to start a podcast," he told me. "And I know exactly what it will be about." I thought his idea was great.

We approached the higher-ups at our radio show and sold them on the concept, with Rafer as host and me as producer. They agreed to let us make a pilot centering on a movie called *Frozen* that would be hitting theaters in a few weeks. (To be clear: not the animated *Frozen* with singing and a softhearted talking snowman but a horror movie about three friends who get trapped on a ski lift for days while wild wolves wait for them to jump to the ground, because apparently wolves love to eat skiers.)

I did some sleuthing and found a man who'd been stuck on a ski lift for twelve hours. Days would have been better, but hey, half a day was still a long time. He agreed to let Rafer interview him. I then got advance screening copies of *Frozen* and sent one to the guest, while Rafer and I watched the other copy. It was an absolutely horrible movie, but that made the prospect of the podcast even more exciting. After all, aren't bad movies always more fun to talk about than good ones?

But then it came time for the taping. Sadly, it was pretty boring.

"What did you do on the ski lift for twelve hours?"

"Just waited."

"Did you pee your pants?"

"No, I peed, but not my pants."

"How realistic was the wolf aspect of the movie?"

"Not at all."

You get the picture.

Our higher-ups were not pleased. But they had an idea: "Rafer, Kristen, why don't you two just host a show together?"

They'd heard Rafer and me talk about movies in the office and loved how much we disagreed and laughed. They liked that Rafer was into action movies and that I was into rom-coms. They said that we could have the occasional "real person" segment on our new show, but that they mostly wanted us to review new movies each week, with our personalities front and center.

In their words: "The show will be a film review podcast focused on new releases, hosted by two friends—male and female—who disagree a lot, and laugh even more."

And so began Movie Date, from WNYC. The show ran for six years, and over time it evolved to also include a number of other segments—not just the film reviews and real-person interviews but also celebrity interviews, movie trivia, and our audio advice column for film lovers, Movie Therapy.

Yes, someone could, if they wanted, say our show was simply about movies. But for any advertiser, higher-up, or press outlet, our show was about more than a one-word answer. Remember how the higher-ups described what they wanted Movie Date to be: "a film review podcast focused on new releases, hosted by two friends—male and female—who disagree a lot, and laugh even more."

Without even listening to an episode, one could discern that it would be dual-hosted, fun, and current. At the same time, the description made clear what the show wasn't: It wasn't about the golden age of cinema or studio news; it wasn't a stuffy scholar giving a lecture or two dudes talking about sci-fi.

So think about it: What is your show about?

If your first answer is money, get more specific ("My podcast is a show that gives novice investors steps for entering and succeeding in the stock market." Or, "My show features concrete tips for people who want to retire by the time they're forty.").

If your first answer is love, think more specifically about what aspect of love you'll be focusing on ("In my podcast, I interview real couples about the ups and downs of the first year of marriage." Or,

"My show tells the funniest dating stories from people who are online dating and feeling lost in the process.").

If your first answer is fishing, think about your specific approach to fishing ("In my podcast, I go on fishing trips with famous people while we talk about our best and worst catches." Or, "On my show, I follow a competitive fisherman around the country as he fishes for glory and cash prizes.").

Warning: At this point, some of you will feel inclined to write five paragraphs about what your show is about. As an exercise, that's totally fine. In fact, it's highly recommended. Go for it!

But after doing that I want you to distill your idea into one, two, three sentences max. These sentences should explain the concept of the show, including what makes it novel.

Then, get used to saying it out loud. Make it sound snappy! Deliver the concept with joy. You have a concrete show idea. And just as important: For your future marketing, advertising, and outreach, you now also have an elevator pitch.

What Is an Elevator Pitch?

An elevator pitch is a succinct, snappy, and persuasive pitch for a product, program, project, and so on. Its name originates from the idea that one should be able to sell an idea to an executive in the time it takes to ride a few floors in the elevator with them. If you can't persuade a higher-up to consider your pitch between the sixth floor and lobby, then your presentation is presumably unclear or unexciting (even if your idea is excellent).

4

Find Inspiration in the Right Places

Back in the days when I dreamed of being the next great American novelist/activist-poet, my teachers said one thing over and over again: "A great writer must also be a great reader." And by this, they meant that creativity isn't a one-way street. To write great words, one must also read great words; and more than anything, one must love the written word.

Fortunately, most writers I've met over the years (or read interviews with) list a wide range of favorite authors—Alice Walker, Ernest Hemingway, Celeste Ng, Gabriel García Márquez, James Baldwin, Zora Neale Hurston, Carson McCullers, John Steinbeck, Haruki Murakami, Edith Wharton, Zadie Smith, Yaa Gyasi. The list is incredibly varied and goes on and on (fortunately, I've yet to come across anyone who's read the iambic pentameter anti-war poems I wrote for my high school literary journal).

In the case of podcasting, however, I've found something different. Nearly half the people who pitch podcast ideas to me list the same handful of shows as their primary source of inspiration or aspiration: This American Life, Radiolab, and Serial.

Note: All three of these are outstanding, award-winning shows and boast huge audiences. Also note: All three are productions of public radio.

Now, let me make something clear: I love public radio. My audio career (and that of many other professional podcasters) began in public radio. Public radio knows how to tell smart, compelling, beautifully produced stories. And yes, many of us who've worked in public radio still let those old sensibilities enter into our storytelling (either deliberately or inadvertently).

But that doesn't mean public radio is what we should all be emulating. In fact, I'm going to argue here that you look elsewhere for inspiration. Here's why:

- Only thirty million people listen to public radio in an average week. If you want to attract new audiences, shouldn't you be looking at all the other things people are consuming instead of public radio and draw inspiration from those things?

- Considering how many aspiring podcasters out there are trying to emulate public radio, shouldn't you be trying to stand out by making something different?

- Doesn't it sound like fun to make something that's totally unlike anything else on the airwaves? Of course it does!

Here are some examples of shows that have taken inspiration from outside the public radio realm:

- The Walk: An immersive fiction podcast by Naomi Alderman, it began as a fitness app by the game company Six to Start, funded by the British National Health Service, and was adapted into a podcast. By listening, you become the main character (code name "Walker") in a first-person suspense adventure. Your mission: to walk secret information across national borders as all the other characters talk to you, guide you, and sometimes deceive you.

- Why Oh Why: a podcast that explores the intersections of love and technology. Host Andrea Silenzi constantly looks for inspiration in unexpected places, blurring the lines between fiction and nonfiction, voyeurism and confessional. In the show's blind Skype dates, listeners nominate themselves to be set up on blind dates and agree to be recorded. For listeners, it's like eavesdropping on someone else's Tinder date.

- 36 Questions: Over the course of the show's three parts, an estranged couple, played by Jonathan Groff and Jessie Shelton, look at what's right and wrong in their relationship and determine whether they should stay together by asking each other 36 questions. A musical drama with only two players, it takes its name from a real social experiment designed to bring two people closer together.

Where else should we be looking for inspiration?

- YouTube
- Snapchat
- video games
- Netflix
- professional sports

There really are no limits! So look all around you: at your grocery store checkout line, at your house of worship, as you walk your dog and attend your next social gathering. What do you see that inspires you? What do you want to spend more time doing? And how would you turn that thing into ear candy?

What Americans Are Actually Consuming

Yes, thirty million listeners tuned in to NPR programming in 2017 in an average week (Pew Research Center, June 6, 2018). But compare that to:

- **TV:** Americans watch more than 7 hours and 50 minutes of TV per household per day (Alexis C. Madrigal, *The Atlantic,* May 30, 2018).

- **NETFLIX:** 139 million people subscribe to Netflix worldwide (Netflix letter to shareholders, January 17, 2019).

- **YOUTUBE:** Worldwide, people watch over one billion hours of YouTube videos every day (Rich McCormick, YouTube Official Blog, February 27, 2017).

5

Be Honest About How Much Love You Have to Give

Friends, I know you have a lot of love in your hearts. You have love for your besties. You have love for late-night marathons of *The Golden Girls*. You have love for that corgi that just passed you on the street. There is no doubt that you're a sweet, loving person. But how much love do you actually have to invest in a podcast?

I'm asking you this because the painful fact is that it's hard to keep a podcast going, and I'll say it here (and I'll say it repeatedly): The one thing that's guaranteed to kill any podcast—more than equipment failures or a shortage of money or not enough time—is a lack of love.

On free podcast hosting sites like Anchor, only 16 percent of podcasts have published more than nine episodes (according to Chartable's hosting data in 2018). That means that the majority of people embarking on podcasting are either choosing to make very-short-run series, or they're giving up after nine episodes.

Based on all the conversations I've had with aspiring podcasters over the years, I'm going to place my bets on the latter being the case 99 percent of the time. And that's not because aspiring podcasters are lazy or bad at podcasting. Most are smart, funny, hardworking people! My theory is that those nine episodes speak to a lack of love for what they're making.

Now, I know love can be a hard thing to gauge. As someone who's fallen in love a million times with guys I've met on Tinder or at bars or at parties—only to wake up the next morning and think, *Why did I kiss that guy? And what was his name?*—I get it.

Love can feel intense, but it can also feel fleeting. That's part of the fun of love. But it absolutely cannot be fleeting when you're making a podcast. And so, as unsexy as it sounds, I urge all aspiring podcasters to look at their show the same way they would a senior college thesis, and ask themselves: Do I love this topic enough to research it and talk about it and dream about it in all my spare time? Do I love the intended outcome enough to work on it hour after hour, week after week, and present it a year from now?

If the idea of a college thesis sounds too horrible, go at things from a different angle: Think about what you're most obsessed with already—whether it's *The Real Housewives,* like Casey Wilson and Danielle Schneider of the Bitch Sesh podcast, or eating, like Dan Pashman of The Sporkful. In both cases, they'd be thinking, talking, and dreaming about those particular topics, regardless of whether they had a podcast.

Either way, your show has to be something you can obsess over and that makes your heart sing. It has to be something you can see yourself doing for more than a weekend or a few weekends. It's the least your heart—and your show—deserve.

So as you continue to read this book and learn more about what it takes to make a great show, do some soul-searching. Think hard about your podcast and how it will fit into your life. Ideally, you'll come to realize that your podcast is way better than a college paper or your favorite hobby—hopefully it will be more like the elderly cat you fell in love with at the Humane Society: the one you know you can dedicate time to, even though you're already spread thin; the one you can't wait to get home to every day to share your love with.

Part 2

WRITE IT

6

Decide on a Format

Format: It's not just for guys named Matt.

Ha! Get it? For . . . Matt!

Oh, how I love a bad pun. But seriously: Format is for everyone. Matt, Elizabeth, Jose, Abraham, Priyanka, and absolutely anyone else who wants to start a podcast.

Very likely, you already know what a format is in the TV world. For example:

* situation comedy (*Friends, Modern Family, Black-ish*)
* police procedural (*Criminal Minds, Law & Order, Cagney & Lacey*)
* game show (*The Price Is Right, Deal or No Deal, Family Feud*)
* daily news program (*NBC Nightly News, The Rachel Maddow Show*)
* reality show competition (*The Bachelor, The Biggest Loser, The Amazing Race*)
* reality show observation (*Keeping Up with the Kardashians, The Real Housewives of New York City*)

In the podcasting world, many of the same formats exist (though fictional storytelling formats—like police procedurals and situation comedies—have yet to attract the large audiences that TV shows have). Here are some of the most common formats in podcasting:

- **interview:** The host welcomes a different guest in each episode, and then asks the guest questions related to the theme of the show (WTF with Marc Maron, Girlboss Radio with Sophia Amoruso).

- **roundtable:** an opinionated roundtable of three hosts (sometimes four, though I consider that too crowded) who discuss, with some disagreement, topics related to the show's theme (*Slate*'s Culture Gabfest, Lovett or Leave It).

- **daily news:** The host reads the news of the day, often turning to reporters for on-the-ground reporting or additional context (The Daily; Start Here; Today, Explained).

- **list:** The host(s) goes through a top five list, a worst-of list, or a list of people they would "date, marry, or make disappear" (Top Five).

- **advice:** The host(s) offers advice to people who write or call in (Car Talk, Dear Prudence, Savage Lovecast).

- **recap:** Episodes of a specific TV show or podcast are recapped by superfans (Watch What Crappens, Serial Serial, Little House on the Podcast, Gilmore Guys).

- **episodic documentary:** Each episode looks closely at a different story, including all its ups and downs, little-known facts, and surprises (Revisionist History).

* **seasonal documentary:** A single story is told in multiple episodes over the course of a season (Dirty John, Heaven's Gate, You Must Remember This).

* **investigation:** The host of the show acts as an investigator in a case or in multiple cases, laying out the mystery and coming to some conclusion about guilt, innocence, and the truth of what happened (Serial, Mystery Show, Missing Richard Simmons).

* **magazine:** Each act of the show is a different stand-alone documentary, interview, performance, or investigation, often related to the overall theme of the specific episode (This American Life, Radiolab).

* **game show:** Guests answer questions, face a series of challenges, unravel puzzles, or play other games in order to come out on top (Ask Me Another, Wait Wait Don't Tell Me).

* **narrated short story(ies):** The host tells a story from beginning to end. Alternatively, multiple short stories are read by multiple readers. The stories may be a piece of short fiction, confessional, diary entry, or monologue (Levar Burton Reads, Selected Shorts, The Moth, Mortified).

* **serial fiction:** A fictional story is told over the course of multiple episodes. In some cases, the podcast creates an imaginary world that releases ongoing dispatches with no foreseeable

end (Welcome to Night Vale). In others it tells a story from beginning to end (The Message, Homecoming).

While successful shows exist in all of the above formats (and many more!), that doesn't mean you have to choose a traditional format. You might even want to make up your own.

For example, in each episode of Beautiful Stories from Anonymous People, comedian Chris Gethard opens the phone line to one anonymous caller. What happens next can be anything from blatant self-promotion to haunting confessional. The only rule is that Chris can't hang up first. Is it an interview show? A storytelling show? A reality show? I'd say it's all of the above and something else entirely.

And consider Everything Is Alive. In each episode, Ian Chillag interviews an inanimate object. Is it an interview show? Fiction? Performance art? Again, I'd say it's all of the above, and also something entirely new.

Or Ear Hustle. Produced at San Quentin State Prison by inmates Earlonne Woods (now out of prison) and Antwan Williams, along with Nigel Poor, the show tells stories of prison life, interwoven with personal narratives and perspectives on social justice. Is it a reality show? A documentary? Investigative journalism? I think Ear Hustle is all of these things, and also something much bigger and truly transcendent.

There are no limits. Choose an existing format. Steal a format that exists in another medium. Make up one of your own. You really can do anything. I believe in you!

The Importance of Story

Many years ago, I had the pleasure of meeting Himan Brown, the legendary radio producer behind The Thin Man, Inner Sanctum, Flash Gordon, Dick Tracy, and many other classic shows. Brown was known for a lot of things: his ability to work well with very famous people (Gregory Peck, Frank Sinatra, Helen Hayes, and Orson Welles, to name just a few), his prolific output (in seven decades he produced more than thirty thousand shows), and, most memorably for me, his insistence that story was at the heart of any great audio production. To paraphrase what he told me: "Meet any child, in any culture, and what will they request of the adults around them? They'll say, 'Tell me a story.' Go anywhere in the world and I promise you this is true. People, from the time we can talk or understand language, long for stories. We want stories, and we need them."

Whatever the format of your show, I beg you to keep Himan Brown's wisdom in the front of your mind. Talk in stories, not facts. Illustrate what you're saying with visually rich words, not just numbers and dates. Draw listeners in by delivering human feelings and experiences and actions. As much as possible, show, don't tell. Whether you're making a game show or a news show or an investigative podcast, give the people what they want. Be a storyteller.

For more on this, turn to Chapter 9: Prepare to Script (page 49).

7

Create a Structure

Congratulations! You've made it to one of my favorite parts of new show development: structure!

Now, you might be thinking: *Why do I need structure? So many shows I love are just fun people talking!*

I'm going to counter by saying that "fun banter" without structure is *not* fun, especially for new listeners who have no idea who you are. And more likely than not, the show you think has no structure actually does.

For example, I co-hosted a show for about six months called When Meghan Met Harry: A Royal Weddingcast. For fans of the British royals, it was a frothy lovefest in which James Barr (a pale redhead from the UK) and I (a woman of color in the United States) subtly reflected the identity of the couple while also celebrating everything about them.

But look closer and you'll see the show wasn't just a lovefest with a carefully selected pair of hosts. It had a solid structure.

Each episode began with James and me introducing ourselves. We'd then give a brief rundown (or "table of contents," as the audio world calls it) explaining what would be coming up in the show. Example:

"Today we'll be talking about the latest headlines, doing a deep dive into divorce in the royal family, and then wrapping up with this week's royal wedding prediction, which has something to do with horses." The table of contents orients listeners while also getting them excited about what will be coming down the path.

Each of the table of contents' teasers is an "act" in the show. After getting past the intro and table of contents, our show had three acts:

Act 1: News

James and I would read three to five of the week's juiciest headlines related to the couple or the wedding. These headlines might be about appearances that they made that week, details about the wedding venue, or a bit of gossip related to one of their families. In all the headlines, we celebrated the couple's love and bemoaned anyone who didn't think they were the most important couple who ever walked the planet.

Act 2: Deep Dive

The deep dive was a closer look at an issue related to Meghan, Harry, or the royals. One week, we might look at the history of race relations in the royal family or at fascinators or wedding food. Another week we'd talk to Harry's old military buddies or Meghan's friends or royal biographers who also happened to be superfans.

Act 3: Royal Wedding Prediction

The show always concluded with a prediction about the royal wedding day itself. It could be the name of a guest (Serena Williams, yes!) or the physical state of a guest (Pippa Middleton will be pregnant!) or something about how the bride would look (boy, were we wrong about her hair). On the big day, we released all our predictions in the form of a bingo board/drinking game that thousands of fans around the world played along with.

Beyond the three acts of When Meghan Met Harry, there were also these structural elements:

- **music:** Each act was marked by signature music specific to the act.
- **time:** Each episode clocked in at about twenty-five minutes.
- **tone:** Every episode was upbeat, doting, and completely unironic.

Now, you might be thinking: *I don't want to be restricted by such a stiff structure!* Or, *I don't see the point!*

But please, trust me on this one: Structure is something to be grateful for, not to resent. A structure gives you a road map. It provides the basic nuts and bolts of what your show sounds like. It gives your listeners a place and space that they're comfortable in. It provides listeners with both predictability ("Yay, I know how this goes!") and surprises ("Oh my gosh, they deviated from what they normally do!"). It provides a place for you to put teasers and a cliffhanger. And if you're lucky enough to have advertisers, your structure provides exact spots where your ads can go.

Now, note: The structure of When Meghan Met Harry is by far the simplest sort of show structure there is. Simple isn't bad. But it may not be for you. You might want to do something more complicated, like what Jolenta and I did when we created By the Book.

Here's the structure of By the Book, in detail:

1. introduction: These are our names, this is our show, this is the book of the week

2. theme song
3. biography of the week's author
4. summary of the week's book
5. the steps of the book we'll be following, in detail

(Note: We try our best to fit all the above parts into the first six minutes of the show.)

6. Jolenta's first week of living by the book, including audio diaries (six minutes)
7. Kristen's first week of living by the book, including audio diaries (six minutes)

—Music bump / ad break—

8. Jolenta's second week of living by the book, including audio diaries (six minutes)
9. Kristen's second week of living by the book, including audio diaries (six minutes)

—Music bump / ad break—

10. Jolenta's verdict on the book (three minutes)
11. Kristen's verdict on the book (three minutes)
12. closing credits, with music
13. Easter egg (a funny outtake that our producers put at the end of each episode as a surprise for us and the listeners).

After several seasons of making By the Book, Jolenta and I barely even think about the structure anymore. It's a perfectly formed universe in which our show can flourish. But it didn't start out that way. Along with Cameron and our managing producer, Mia Lobel, we did a lot of experimentation before landing on our structure as it currently exists, and you might, as well. In our case, it took months.

But once we had it down, the subsequent episodes were relatively easy to make. We knew where every part of the story belonged, and on the odd occasion when we deviated from the structure, it was clear to our listeners what we were doing and why.

Additionally, our structure gave the show what audio people call a "clock." A clock lays out how long each part of the show should be, and in doing so gives the show a tempo. In our case, it also helped us to know how much tape to gather, the pace at which our story arcs should progress, and how long each episode should time out at (approximately forty minutes).

Now, think about your own show's structure. Use your imagination. Think of it as the blueprint for your dream home. The home can look any way you want it to, but it needs good bones, and you get to decide where those bones belong. Once you have a rough idea of your show's shape, try doing a practice run of your show. Note the places where your show lags, and where it comes alive. What feels fun when you're doing it, and what feels like a chore?

Go back to the drawing board, rework the structure, then rework it again. I promise you that, with time, you'll have your dream home.

8

Focus on the Top

I'm going to confess something to you: During the piloting process of By the Book, we made some pretty bad versions of the show. They dragged, they stumbled, they sounded like a mess, and the very worst part of these early attempts was the top of the show.

In the beginning, our introductions were fifteen minutes or longer. In that time, we introduced ourselves, our personalities, our personal histories, how we met, how we're different, how we're the same. And then we'd get into the week's book, the experience of reading it, the biography of the author, the extremely detailed breakdown of the rules—it just went on and on. Some very honest friends and colleagues confessed that they were bored stiff by it all. Yes, they wanted to know the lay of the land, but more than anything, they wanted to get to the action. They wanted to hear Jolenta and me living by self-help books, rather than just talking about them.

So, we reworked the top of the show, and then reworked it again. After lots of experimentation, we managed to get all the introductions to comfortably fit into the first five to six minutes of the debut episode.

That included introducing us, the book, the author of the book, the rules of the book, everything.

And, despite being a comedy show, we made the decision to present all the introductory components in a straightforward, neutral fashion. Part of this was so listeners would have no idea of whether we liked or hated the books—anticipation is good! And part of this was so we wouldn't alienate the self-help lovers or the self-help haters—we wanted them both!

Now, this may seem like a lot of effort to put into such a tiny little part of the show. But I must tell you something, and I beg you to commit it to memory: The first five minutes of a podcast episode are crucial. According to 2016 data from NPR One, podcasts typically lose 20 to 35 percent of listeners within the first five minutes. In fact, the listener drop-off rate is higher in the first five minutes of an episode than at any other time.

So, while it might seem bonkers to spend fifty hours mastering the first five minutes of your pilot episode, I guarantee that those fifty hours will pay off.

My Beef with Endless Top-of-the-Show Banter

Some podcast hosts make the mistake of chatting and laughing and catching up with each other for ten, twenty, or even thirty minutes at the top of their show. The hosts are good friends, and they presume their listeners are good friends. Who doesn't just like to talk for hours with good friends? The answer: new listeners.

Allow me to illustrate:

Have you ever gone to a party where you knew almost nobody there? Maybe a friend invited you to her friend's party. You showed up, but your friend was running late. And so, you did your best to be social. You approached one of the little circles of strangers talking, but no one in the circle acknowledged you. Instead, they just went right on talking. You surmised that baking was important to them, or maybe that royalty was. But they didn't bother to welcome you at any point or bring you up to speed on the conversation. You felt alienated and wondered if maybe you should just pretend to be sick, leave the party, and go home and watch TV instead.

This is what endless top-of-the-show banter feels like to a lot of new listeners. You, the hosts, are having fun with each other, and your old listeners are probably also having a good time, but new listeners have no idea who you are or what you're talking about and wonder whether they're even welcome at your party.

The simple solution: Keep top-of-the-show banter brief. Then, do what you would if a person approached your circle at a party: Say, "Hello, my name is Jeff, this is Susan, and we were just talking about why oatmeal raisin cookies are the king of cookies, despite the popular belief that chocolate chip cookies wear the crown."

Too much banter without acknowledging your guests is a lousy way to host—whether at a party or on your podcast. Be the good host that we all know you are! Let everyone know they're welcome!

9

Prepare to Script

Sooner or later, you're going to need a script. In some cases, the script will come during the planning and dreaming phase—it will be an integral part of your brainstorming and central to how you imagine and reimagine your show sounding. In others, it will come much later, in the making phase—after you've gathered other audio components and done other legwork. But regardless, I want you to consider right now what kind of script you'll need and what makes for a good script.

In the case of many shows, you'll only need a minimal script—or, to be more accurate, an outline. For example, consider a show that's in list style. We'll call this imaginary show Top Five Wrestlers of the Week. It's possible that your outline will just include your introduction, a list of five wrestlers, two reasons under each wrestler about why they're tops this week, and then a conclusion.

Another example of a show that may require only an outline is a roundtable show. (Think *Slate*'s The Waves, which I've guest-hosted several times.) The outline usually just includes an introduction at the top of the show, the table of contents, the names of the panelists, the three topics of the day, some notable points under each topic, then the conclusion.

Shows that rely on outlines have a lot of advantages over shows that have fully fleshed-out scripts. They have more room for improvisation and surprises. They allow for the hosts to show off their personalities and play off each other. And they require less writing!

But that doesn't mean there's no planning or work. In some ways, you have to be even more prepared when you don't have a script, because it's on you to fill in all the gaps in your outline. That means you have to do plenty of research and reading and note-taking in advance. It means you have to know before your recording date where you stand on an issue and why (after all, you're not just going to make up reasons why certain wrestlers rocked your world this week, right?). It means there won't be any words in front of you to catch you if you fumble.

But then there are some shows that most certainly do need a detailed script, in which the hosts read most of what's on the page word for word. For example:

- Shows that are time-sensitive and news-driven, whether hard news or pop culture news, like The Daily or Up First. These shows don't just rely upon a lot of facts; the facts might change throughout the day or week, so it's important to make sure they're updated regularly.

- Shows involving tape that you've captured outside the studio. Think Revisionist History or Mystery Show. Of all the tape you gathered in the making of an episode, what clips are actually going to be included in the show? What story does the tape tell, and what will you say between each clip to continue to drive the story forward? What transitions will be required as you go in and out of each clip?

- Shows that are audio plays, fiction, crafted reality shows.

- Shows that tell a detailed lesson or history, like You Must Remember This and Unladylike. These shows deliver lots of facts, and a script is necessary to make sure all these important bits are covered in a clear way.

Let's walk through each of these kinds of show scripts, so that I can give you a bit of advice on what I consider most important in each one.

News shows: Follow the journalism rule "Don't bury the lede." By that I mean, don't do a long, flowery, confusing introduction into the third-least-important story of the day at the top of your show and assume your listeners will be able to follow you (or want to, for that matter). Start with the big story, make clear what the headline is, then give details that listeners can actually visualize. And make sure before all that to include the table of contents mentioned in the structure chapter!

Shows with lots of tape gathered outside the studio: "Write to the tape" is a term a lot of us use in audio, and it means that you need to let the tape you collect tell the story for you. A lot of newbies will begin by deciding the story they want to tell first, writing a whole script next, and then collecting some interview clips to drop into the script to illustrate their points at the end. This is doing things in the wrong order.

Yes, you should have some sense of the story you want to tell first, but your next step is then to collect the audio that will tell your story for you—that means conversations, expert interviews, and so on. After you have all your tape, I highly recommend getting it transcribed with a service like Trint (though it's also possible to listen through all your tape multiple times while taking notes, or transcribe the audio on your own). Then, look through your transcripts and notes and choose the clips that illustrate with clarity everything your story is about and write the narration lines around those clips.

Audio plays, fiction, crafted reality shows: Take risks. To paraphrase my friend Ann Heppermann, who founded the Sarah Awards for Audio Fiction, "Challenge the way you think about audio, and push the boundaries of what audio can and should be." The beauty of a podcast is that you can create a whole universe without million-dollar sets or theater rental fees. Think of Welcome to Night Vale and Homecoming. Both shows have unique worlds, with their own audio-vocabularies, where strange things happen.

Lessons and history: I cannot state enough how important it is that you are not delivering a research paper. The temptation will be to pack in a bunch of facts, dates, names, and so on. But remember, your listeners aren't just there for the facts. If they want facts and nothing else, they can read an encyclopedia. They want a story.

And this gets to an important point for every podcaster out there, regardless of what kind of script you're writing: Your job is to be an outstanding storyteller. On the surface, it may look like you're just relaying information or having a conversation. But as a podcaster, you're doing much more: You're giving your listeners something that hits them in the heart and brain via those holes in the sides of their heads. Your script should reflect that. So find the arc in each story you're telling, or create it. Play up what's exciting, and give gravity to what's serious. Make things come alive.

As you do all this, be mindful to always write for the ear, not for the eye—in other words, write for an audience that's listening, not reading. At the same time, write for a host who is speaking, not consuming words with their eyes. This is something that a lot of print journalists, academics, and writers struggle with at first (myself included). That's because in most traditional writing forms, the words are not meant to be consumed audibly or vocalized. But podcasting is different.

Consider this sentence: "A popular accordionist and jazz flute performer at local cafes in his college days, John Smith, now thirty-two, has entered a new phase in his life that is not uncommon among aspiring musicians over the age of thirty—a phase marked by a desire for stability and the sad realization that international fame and fortune may not be in the cards."

Try to read that sentence out loud. How many times did you pause to take deep breaths? How many times did you trip over the words? What sounded clunky? Did any of it sound natural?

The fact is, that sentence works just fine in print, but it does not work in audio. When you're writing for the ear, you also have to write for the breath. That means aiming for shorter, punchier sentences. It means choosing words with fewer syllables. It means talking in more straight lines and fewer circles.

Now, let's rewrite that sentence into several shorter, punchier sentences: "John Smith was an accordionist and jazz flute performer who was locally popular in his college days. But that was more than a decade ago. Smith is now thirty-two. And like a lot of musicians his age, his priorities are shifting. He longs for stability. At the same time, he's coming to terms with the fact that international fame and fortune may not be in the cards."

Better, yes? Easier to read out loud, easier to follow with the ear.

It just takes practice. So write, write some more, then do rewrites. Speak your scripts out loud as you write them. Use table reads (see next page) as a chance to improve what's on the page. Even when you're in the studio taping, stop if you need to in order to rewrite sentences that sound unnatural or stiff coming out of your mouth (unless your show is titled Robots Read Poetry—in that case, unnatural and stiff is probably what you're aiming for).

Above all, be sure to make your scripts sound like you and your personality. That means incorporating your sense of humor, personal asides, unique vocabulary, and particular turns of phrase.

It's your show, my friends. Make it sound like you.

What Is a Table Read?

A table read is like a cross between a rehearsal and a workshop for an episode. In most table reads, the hosts of a show will have a script in front of them, as well as audio clips cued up to be played at the appropriate times. As they read through an entire episode's script and hear the clips, the hosts (and often a full production team) will take notes on what's working and what's not—including clarity, tempo, tone, clunkiness, and more. The notes are usually shared at the end of the read. The script is then reworked, and new clips are sometimes chosen. Some clips or sections may be cut entirely. Not all shows can afford the time and team to do an in-depth table read, but the shows that do are invariably better for the process.

10

Give Your Show a Strong Title

Maybe you've had a title in mind all along for your show, or maybe you're just starting to create a short list of titles now that you know more about what your show is going to sound like.

I personally like to come up with titles later, not earlier. That's because I think it's important to know the thing I'm describing before I describe it (the "thing" in this case being the podcast, and the description being the title).

Now, I'm sure your dream title is terrific. And in an ideal world, I'd just say, "Name your show whatever you like! Any title is fine!" But our world is not ideal. So before you settle on a title, do the following:

- See what else is out there. There are more than a million podcasts in the world, and some may already have the name you want. To find out what you're competing with, do a Google search on your preferred podcast name, along with the word "podcast," and see what comes up. Also do a search in Apple Podcasts and other podcast apps. If there are shows with the same title as yours, but the shows haven't been in production for years, then you're probably safe to use the title yourself. But if there's another show that's actively putting out episodes now with your title or some other similar project or product using your title, I'd suggest you find a new title, for two reasons: 1) so that your potential listeners aren't confused about which show is yours and 2) to avoid a potential intellectual property rights squabble (the rules around all this are still being written, as podcasting is a relatively new medium, but better safe than sorry).

* Keep your title snappy. Shows that have ten-word titles are hard to memorize and don't roll off the tongue. And on top of that, they don't fit well on the show tile (also known as your show art or show icon) or in the Apple search window. So make your title brief, memorable, and easy to say.

* Make sure your title relays what your show is about. I recently came across a show with a title that was similar to "By the Book," but oddly, it was a show about movies. I was perplexed. Why would a show about movies have a reference to books in its title? And this isn't the first time I've stumbled across this confusing situation. I've seen it with food shows, TV recap shows, music shows, and more. Don't make the same mistake! Not only will a confusing title make your show harder to promote, it will alienate the people who genuinely want to hear about the topic you're actually discussing.

Part 3

HOST IT

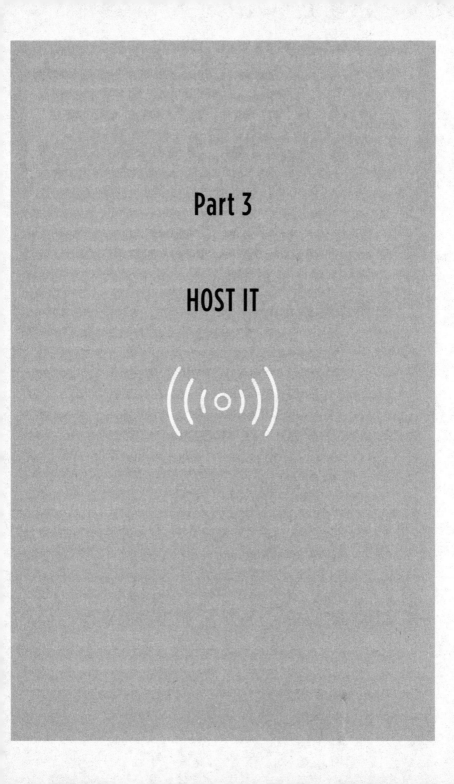

11

Think About Diversity

We've talked a lot about ideas up until now. But we're about to jump into several chapters that talk about people: the people who host your show, the people who are guests on your show, the people who produce your show. And when it comes to any conversation about people and podcasting, it's absolutely necessary that we talk about diversity.

Now, I know that "diversity" can feel like a dirty word. For those of us who are minorities, it can sometimes make us feel like "Great, I'm here to represent my entire race/gender/religion/other status." And for folks in more dominant positions (white people, men, straight people, and so on) engaging diversity can feel uncomfortable at best, exhausting and useless at worst.

But trust me, diversity is something every show needs. Consider this:

1. A diverse team differentiates you. Sixty-six percent of podcasts have a white male host. And every time another white man chooses to host a show without people of color as

contributors, without women as co-hosts, and so on, there's the potential for him to blend in with or sound like an imitation of the status quo.

2. A diverse team means the potential to reach more listeners. Remember, the vast majority of people in America are not white men. Why not make a conscious effort to appeal to the majority by including their voices either as guests, co-hosts, or regular on-air contributors?

3. A diverse team means more diverse sources. It's not easy for everyone to open up to a stranger with a microphone. And it's often even harder when the person with the microphone comes from a completely different world. For example, if you're a black woman who's living with ovarian cancer, do you really want to run to a white man first with your story? Maybe you do. But maybe you'd rather tell your story to someone whose identity is a bit more like your own.

4. A diverse team means fewer blind spots. When there's a lack of diversity, there's a greater likelihood of only seeing things through one lens, or presuming that something is a given that actually isn't. For example, if you're on a team of straight people making a show about marriage, are there going to be presumptions about who traditionally pops the question that don't apply to gay couples? Are there going to be blind spots about the best places to get married when some places are, in fact, not welcoming to gay people?

5. A diverse team means you're part of the solution, not the problem. Our world is full of racism and sexism and ho-

mophobia and loads of other ugly things. And sadly, too many podcasters are making content that perpetuates all that ugliness without even realizing it (or so I hope). For example, how many times have you listened to a roundtable show featuring today's greatest political thinkers—all of whom happen to be men? How many times have you heard shows interview the greatest actors/writers/scientists of our times, only to bring on white guests? This mistake is so common that many "mainstream consumers" don't even question it—but believe me, there are plenty of us who notice and detest it.

These are just a few of the reasons why diversity equals good storytelling and good business. And when I share them with people, they usually nod and say, "This all makes sense!" But then, many of them follow up with me and confess with some embarrassment, "I know diversity is important, but I just don't know how to find diverse people."

If this is you, I promise that you're not alone. This is a perpetual problem in journalism and the media. They are fields that have been dominated by white men for decades. They are fields that have also been dominated by people who are well connected and well to do.

That's partly because networking plays heavily into the media industry. And people tend to network with people who look like them, went to schools like theirs, live in similar neighborhoods, and "speak their language." In an industry that started out skewing white and male, that means a continued trajectory of white and male.

It's also partly due to the fact that the industry has traditionally auditioned new people through unpaid or poorly paid internships. And when internships are unpaid or poorly paid, that means that most low-income people aren't going to pursue them.

And frankly, it has to do with the fact that we live in a world that still puts more trust in white men, that puts white men at the center of stories, that elects white men to office over all other people, and that teaches racism and sexism to us at a very young age.

All that being said, the situation is not hopeless. There are tons of ways to recruit diverse teams! Here are just a few:

- Attend minority networking events or list jobs in minority newsletters. Consider the National Association of Black Journalists, National Association of Hispanic Journalists, Asian American Journalists Association, Native American Journalists Association, UNITY Journalists (coalition of NABJ, NAHJ, AAJA and NAJA), and South Asian Journalists Association.

- Post jobs on public university job boards. Many media organizations I've worked with have habitually recruited only from the "cream of the crop" schools (Ivy League schools and other private universities). In their minds, they're getting the best and brightest, but in reality, they're just getting the richest and whitest. For college grads who are truly diverse in terms of national origin, economic class, race, and perspective, public schools are the way to go.

- Reach out to Facebook communities and ask if you can list job postings or guest requests on their pages. There are thousands of Facebook communities for people of color, women in podcasting, women of color in podcasting, women in media, and so on.

- Look for people in professions that are adjacent to podcasting, like radio, TV, print journalism, publishing, research, and education.

As for recruiting diverse guests, experts, human voices, and so on for your show, look to some of the many lists put together by experts. Among them:

- the Brookings Institution's Women+ in Tech Sourcelist
- the Women's Media Center SheSource list
- *Columbia Journalism Review*'s public database of women, nonbinary people, and people of color who are experts on the media
- NPR's Source of the Week

And above all, practice what I consider the single most important rule for finding diverse guests (and I want you to commit these words to memory): *Google the words you're afraid to Google.*

That means that if you're hosting a show that talks with stay-at-home dads and you realize, "Oh no, all my dads for the past month have been white," Google "black stay-at-home dads," "dads of color," and other phrases that scare you or make you cringe. If you're realizing all the guest slots on your show about science are being filled with white male scientists, Google "black female physicist" or "Asian-American astronaut" or "Latina biologist."

Google those words until it stops being scary. Google them knowing that you're doing the right thing for your show and for the world. Google "black" and "Latino" and "LGBTQ," because none of these are dirty words. Google them because being color blind or color averse is the real dirtiness.

And I promise you that these searches will bring up everything you need: daddy blogs, mommy blogs, professional networking organizations, student groups, official lists, university departments, companies, clubs, and personal web pages. Not all of these pages will be your final destination for finding the diverse people you want, but they may be a first stop where you can find further leads.

I'll have more on the nuts and bolts of getting great (diverse!) guests in Chapter 16, Get the Guests You Want (page 85), so stay tuned!

The Lack of Diversity in Podcasting

In January 2016 Josh Morgan wrote a piece for Quartz titled "Data Confirm That Podcasting in the US Is a White Male Thing." It laid out some grim facts:

- After looking at more than 1,400 podcasts in Apple Podcasts, he found that 85 percent of American podcasts sampled had at least one white host.

- Two-thirds (66 percent) had a white male host.

- Roughly 30 percent had a white female host.

- Only 18 percent of podcasts had a non-white host.

12

Host Like a Pro

I hear one thing over and over again from aspiring hosts—often delivered with shame and embarrassment: "I'm not sure if I have the voice of a podcaster."

I'm going to tell you something here and now: Yes, you absolutely do. And don't let any hosers out there tell you otherwise. And yes, there will be hosers.

Case in point: Jolenta and I host a hugely popular and respected podcast, and yet we still get reviews regularly that say I need to tone down my Minnesota accent and Jolenta needs to eliminate her vocal fry.

My response to both criticisms: baloney.

On the issue of accents: People who don't like the fact that people come from different regions of the country or the world can just shove it. Not everyone should sound like they're from New York or California (the states from which a large percentage of podcast hosts hail). And listeners who think we should are often just harboring a coded form of classism that suggests people from the Midwest and the South are stupid. Am I stupid? No, gentle readers, I am not. And frankly, the charm of a regional accent should not be underestimated.

For every one person who writes in to complain about my Minnesota accent, ten write in to say it reminds them of cookies and grandmas and movies by the Coen brothers.

Now, let's talk vocal fry. This is a subject that I'm particularly prickly about. That's because, as I see it, vocal fry does not exist. Haters will tell you otherwise. In comment threads and even legit newspapers they'll complain about it. Sometimes they'll describe it as the sound of young women speaking at a lower register from the backs of their throats. Alternatively, they'll describe it as a horrible modern mutation of Valley Girl–speak. Less charitably, they'll describe it as the lazy, gravelly voice of a girl who thinks she's too cool for everyone else. More often than not, they'll explain that vocal fry makes a woman's voice sound rough and creaking rather than authoritative and trustworthy. Across the board, they'll insist it makes women sound stupid. And above all, they'll say it makes them never want to listen to a young woman talk again.

Note the common denominator here: It's a criticism of women's voices, particularly those of young women.

Mind you, podcast poster boys like Ira Glass have admitted to doing all the same things with their voices that women accused of vocal fry do—from speaking at a low register to talking in a gravelly voice. But these men never get criticized for it. In fact, Ira admitted in a segment on This American Life titled "Freedom Fries" that every single one of the hundreds of listener letters he's received over the years criticizing contributor voices have targeted women. Every. Single. One.

My point here: If you're a woman and you decide to talk, there will always be haters out there who criticize your voice. Ignore them. Keep using that beautiful voice of yours.

Speaking of Ira Glass, this is a great time to bring up the most important piece of advice I have for all the hosts and aspiring hosts out there. If you take nothing else away from this chapter, please commit this to memory and embroider it on your heart: *Sound like you.*

Not like Ira Glass, not like Phoebe Robinson or Terry Gross, or Jenna Wortham. *You.*

This is tough for a lot of new hosts. They have their favorite shows and want to sound like the people who host those shows. Alternatively, they accidentally find themselves imitating famous hosts without meaning to because their subconscious is telling them, *That's what a professional podcast host sounds like.*

But the truth is that imitation sounds exactly like what it is: fake. No matter how hard you try, you can't sound like Ashley C. Ford or Jad Abumrad. You can only sound like you. And let me reassure you: That's a good thing. No, *that's a great thing.* You are one of a kind. You are a superstar. You are the only one on this planet who is a card-carrying member of you. So please, embrace who you are. That means enjoying your above-mentioned unique accent if you have one, your personal figures of speech, your weird sense of humor, your laughter, and without restraint, your particular point of view.

Now, you might be wondering: *Hey, shouldn't a host be neutral? I don't know if I should deliver opinions!* My answer: That might apply to network news and public radio, but podcasts are neither of these things. Podcasts—even the most informative of them—are entertainment, conversation, and companionship. And that means that podcast audiences want their hosts to be human, to have things they're passionate about, and to have opinions. Even the most neutral-sounding podcasts have hosts who are passionate about their topics—whether the topic is bird-watching or how to be a happier parent. Show your passion!

On the topic of sounding human, that also means—as uncomfortable as it may sound—revealing a bit of vulnerability. I'm not saying you have to cry on every episode of your show, or divulge the most embarrassing fight you've ever had with your spouse. But you should let out some of your flaws and contradictions—whether that's admitting that you don't fold your laundry or laughing about a mistake you made planning for the day's show. Doing so will endear you to your listeners and demonstrate that you're a real honest-to-goodness person just like them.

Now, I said that *sound like you* is the most important thing for you to take away from this chapter, but that doesn't mean it's my only bit of hosting advice. While being yourself, you can also do all of the following:

1. Be prepared. When it's time to sit down at the mic, you should already be familiar with the show script or outline, your opinions on the topics, and how you want to talk about the topics. When you're prepared, you sound more confident and relaxed.

2. Warm up! Do five jumping jacks before recording. Make small talk with your co-host, producer, or yourself. Sing along with a favorite music video. Get your voice and energy ready.

3. Keep water or clear herbal tea on hand, in a closed container. Caffeine-free, dairy-free beverages help your throat and mouth to stay moist, not phlegmy or dry. And closed containers (think: a reusable travel mug) mean you'll never be nervous about spilling on your computer, equipment, or script.

4. Position the mic roughly one fist away from your mouth and slightly toward the left or right side of your mouth. This will keep your voice loud and clear while preventing your *P*'s and *S*'s from popping.

5. Do people often ask you to repeat yourself when you talk with them? If so, you may have a tendency to slur your words together. Work to enunciate your words without over-

correcting or sounding stiff. And keep sipping that water, so your mouth doesn't get sticky.

6. If you say "like" or "um" a lot, do your best to cut back. It's no fun editing out all those "um"s and "uh"s and "like"s when it comes time to put your show together.

7. If your voice lacks energy, find a way to pump it up. Try standing up while you record, smiling while you speak, and using your hands to gesture wildly. Alternatively, consider whether the topic you're discussing is putting you to sleep and choose a topic that excites you instead.

8. Move your mouth slightly away from the mic when you laugh. Laughter is magical, but also tends to be louder than talking, so turning a bit away from the mic will keep your audio more level.

9. If you stumble on something you're saying, don't just start over again from that stumbled word. Start the entire sentence or paragraph over so that it's easier to put things back together again in post production.

10. If you tend to go on tangents, rein it in. Small, occasional tangents are fine, but if you get to the point where you're saying, after a long exhale, "Well . . . like I was saying . . . what was I saying?" that's a problem.

Thank You, Alex Johnson

After ten plus years of speaking on live radio shows, podcasts, stages, and TV programs, I feel pretty at ease with my voice. But it took a lot of practice and the continued cheerleading of people who believed in me to reach this point. One of the most important of these people was Alex Johnson. In my early days as an on-air film critic on the public radio show The Takeaway, I was aware of the fact that I didn't have a "public radio voice." Public radio was a place where people sounded smooth and authoritative. They never seemed to have accents or use unique figures of speech. They were perfect, in my mind, and when I compared myself to them, I always felt like an amateur, or worse, a fraud. And yet, every time I was on air, I returned to my desk to find a GChat or Post-it note on my desk from Alex, the show's digital producer, saying, *You were terrific!* or *You are such a pleasure to listen to!*

I always said thank you, but eventually I confronted him about it. "Alex," I said, "it's so nice of you to try to get my confidence up each week. It really does help, but I know I don't sound like a real public radio person."

Alex's face spread into a giant smile. "Kristen, I'm not trying to build your confidence, I'm just telling you the truth. Yes, you're right, you don't sound like anyone else in the public radio world. You sound just like you, and that's what makes you great."

Hearing those words changed how I felt about my own on-air voice. And after hearing them, I never compared my voice to anyone else's again. I only tried to sound more like me.

13

Consider Getting a Co-Host

I love having a co-host. I love being a co-host. I've been a regular host of three shows in my life—and in each of these shows I've been part of a dynamic duo.

Of course, not every show needs a co-host. Some of my favorite shows in the world (I'm talking to you, Little House on the Podcast) have a single host who makes me laugh and laugh.

But let me walk you through some of the benefits of hosting with someone else versus hosting alone.

The first is that one of you can serve as the foil. In literature, movies, and other forms of entertainment, the foil is a character who contrasts with another character.

One of my favorite examples of a foil can be heard on Happier with Gretchen Rubin. For those who aren't familiar with her, Gretchen Rubin is the hugely popular author of *The Happiness Project* and *Outer Order, Inner Calm,* among other books. On her show, she suggests concrete habit changes people can enlist if they're hoping to be a little happier. Gretchen is disciplined about her habits and often refers to herself as a "happiness bully."

But Gretchen doesn't host her show alone. Along for the ride is her younger sister, Liz Craft. Liz is a screenwriter who talks openly about the messy parts of her life—from her addiction to Candy Crush to her anxiety about Hollywood pitch meetings to her tendency to just throw all her clothes onto her bedroom floor. She has bad habits and isn't always great about enacting the new habits Gretchen suggests.

If you were to summarize their roles in the show, Gretchen would be the happiness guru while Liz would be the stand-in for the typical listener. Together, they're perfectly balanced. They are foils for each other.

But the foil relationship isn't just about bringing balance to a show. Good foils should also highlight each other's differences. Conflict is fun to listen to! Different opinions are intriguing. Think about the typical romantic-comedy duo—they're compatible enough to be drawn to each other but different enough to create sparks. They ask each other tough questions, push each other out of their comfort zones, call each other on their crap, and make each other—and the listeners—laugh.

Another huge benefit of having a co-host relates to diversity. For more on why diversity is important, go back to chapter 11, Think About Diversity (page 59).

Of course, the benefits of co-hosting go beyond diversity and contrast and balance and all those other things experienced by listeners of a show. They also include all the things that happen off mic.

I can say with complete honesty that I'm far better at getting things done when people are counting on me. That includes everything from writing this book (cheers to my editor, Cassie Jones) to getting out of bed in the morning (I'm talking to everyone I've ever worked with here). I hate to disappoint people, and when I'm accountable to someone else—specifically a co-host—I get a lot more done.

Take, for example, By the Book. I love doing all the things that don't relate to the actual production of an episode: coming up with ideas for books to live by, setting up a production schedule, interacting with listeners on social media. But when it comes to doing the actual work of making an episode, I'm not sure I'd do any of it if Jolenta wasn't counting on me.

That's because it's hard to make our show. We have to read a new book cover to cover every two weeks, distill the rules down to five to ten easy-to-understand steps, live by the rules of the books while recording our private lives, and then craft all the audio we collect into a story arc so that we can then go into a studio and record an episode. And that's just to record the first draft.

It's exhausting work! And I don't even have to cut it all together! We have an amazing producer who does all that!

Sometimes it just makes me want to stay in my pajamas and spend all day on Twitter posting cute animal memes. But then I remember: I'm not in this alone, and I'm sure as hell not going to let down my other half. She's counting on me. I'm counting on her. We're in this together.

One final point about the benefits of having a co-host: It's fun. Or, I should say, it's always been fun for me. That's because my co-hosts haven't just motivated me to keep my focus, they've also laughed with me about the silliness of our lives as hosts, soothed me when I'm feeling stressed out, and taught me a ton about being a better host and a better person. I count all my current and former co-hosts as friends, even if they were initially just another talented person I was asked to talk with on mic.

At this point, you may be saying, "Wow, this all sounds great! I think I want a co-host! Why would anyone ever make a show without one?" Then again, you may also be saying, "Oh no, I have zero idea of how to find a co-host. How can I possibly find one?" Not to worry, my friends. I have some suggestions for you:

1. Approach people you've enjoyed working with in the past—
   whether in a professional setting, at a volunteer gig, on

classroom projects, at your house of worship, or in your community. If you worked well together in the past, there's a good chance you'll work well together in the future.

2. Choose a co-host whose work you admire. Perhaps there's someone you've met in a podcasting class, at a podcasting meet-up, or at a conference whose energy you love and who you consider outstanding in their field. Maybe there's a person who used to host a podcast you enjoyed and you want to put your hat in the ring to be their next co-host. Don't be bashful. Ask to meet with them and talk over your ideas.

3. Find a co-host whose skills and identity complement your own rather than match them. Look around. I assure you they're everywhere! For example, if you're a self-taught woodworker who wants to host a show about handicrafts, find a woodwork historian. If you're a comedy lover who wants to host a show about comedy, find someone who actually goes onstage and tells jokes.

4. Don't be afraid to try one co-host, and then try another and another. Network podcasts frequently audition multiple co-hosting pairs to find the two with the best chemistry. Feel free to do the same! Let each potential co-host know up front that you'll be trying to make a pilot with a few different people to see who you sound best with on air. And make clear that if they're not selected, it's not personal, it's really about how well the two of you complement each other.

14

Master the Art of Co-Hosting

I've been very lucky. I've never had to break up with a co-host. And I give all my co-hosts a huge amount of credit for this. They've all been hardworking, patient, top-rate professionals. They've come into most of our tapings prepared. And even if they haven't deliberately set out to do so, they've followed the "yes, and" rule in our shows.

Anyone reading who's familiar with improv comedy knows that the "yes, and" rule is essentially a way of saying, "Wherever you're steering this conversation, I'll go with you." For example, imagine your show is focused on cars, and your topic for the day is cars that get a lot of mileage with very little gas, and your third segment of the show is about electric cars. You and your co-host have each come in with one or two electric cars that you want to talk about in that segment. The thing is, you were hoping to start with your favorite car, the Prius. Meanwhile, your co-host launched things off with her favorite car, the Tesla. If you were petulant and unprofessional, you might yell, "Me first! My car is better!" or "Screw you, if you're going to talk about Teslas, I'm just going to talk about sea lions!" But a host that follows the "yes, and" rule lets the explanation of the Tesla happen, then engages in a conversation about the Tesla's merits and drawbacks before launching into talk about the Prius. Note: I didn't say you have to agree with your co-host about the Tesla. That would be disingenuous and boring. But I did say to go with it. Be a "yes, and" host, not a "no, it's all about me" host.

A lot of this requires that you take turns steering the ship. You can't do all the talking, and neither can your co-host. Aim for balance.

Other tips for successful co-hosting:

1. Know what each of your roles is on the show, or what "characters" you'll play. That means knowing if you're the believer or the skeptic, the liberal or the conservative, the person who's all rules or the person who's a free spirit. For example, when Rafer and I were hosting Movie Date, he was the professional film critic and I was the stand-in for general film-loving audiences. Personality-wise, I was the one who laughed a lot (so much that some listeners criticized me). He was the one who was more businesslike.

2. Determine what your roles in the show's production are, and switch up those roles if need be. For example, I usually write the book summary and author bio in our scripts for By the Book in addition to my own story. Jolenta writes her own story. Together, we write out the rules. Jolenta writes all of our pickup scripts (the scripts we use for the second taping of each episode, which includes corrections and additional information as needed).

3. Plan, plan, plan. Know in advance what you'll be talking about in each episode. Map it out beforehand. Don't show up to record with no idea of what you're going to say or what

you'll each be bringing to the table. It will only lead to conflict.

4. Pull your own weight. Yes, there will be times when one of you does more than the other, but if those times are more than occasional, strife is going to build up. Don't let it! Talk it through, come up with new ways to stay on top of your tasks, or consider reworking what tasks each of you does.

5. Treat your co-host as a partner, not an adversary. That means putting your ego on the back burner, communicating about what's working and what's not, and doing what you can to make each other look good.

15

Deal with Co-Host Conflict

Now, as I said, I've been really lucky with my co-hosts. They've all been outstanding professionals and humans. But not all hosts have been so lucky. I've been witness to some of these co-hosting disasters.

In one case, the male host of the show was—how can I put this nicely?—oh yeah, he was a total raging asshole. He was simultaneously convinced he was the smartest person in the room at all times and terrified that anyone sharing the mic with him might steal his thunder. On air, he talked over his co-hosts and interrupted their interviews with "better questions" and "corrections." Off air, he complained about them and refused to collaborate. Note that I said "co-hosts," plural. That's because he went through three co-hosts in quick succession.

This guy was completely unprofessional in a million ways. He didn't treat his co-hosts like partners; he attacked them like enemies. Now, this is a pretty extreme example. There are also more subtle versions of incompatibility.

For example, some friends just shouldn't co-host. I know, I know.

You guys are besties. You are so on the same page with your world-views and you never get tired of spending time together! But even if your podcast is "just a hobby," it's still a business. And starting a business with a friend can be dangerous. What if one of you has a work style that drives the other nuts? What if one of you is a class-A procrastinator and the other gets all the work done without being asked? What if one of you is always on time, and the other has a more relaxed relationship with clocks? What if one of you is great with money and the other is, well, a little less good with it?

Of course, I have to remind readers here that I co-host By the Book with a friend: the great Jolenta Greenberg. But Jolenta and I didn't start off that way. By that I mean we started off years ago as co-workers, clocking in on the same show at the same radio station. Because we were co-workers before friends before co-hosts, we knew each other's strengths and weaknesses. We knew each other's workplace communications styles. We knew how we handled timelines and deadlines. And we knew we liked working with each other. Thus, when she first approached me about co-hosting By the Book with her, I went in pretty confident about our ability to work well together. Fortunately, that confidence has been rewarded over and over again.

My advice before choosing to work with any co-host: Think of all the worst-case scenarios that can happen in making a show, and how each of you would handle those situations. Also, think of the mundane, everyday stuff that's got to be done—from answering emails to doing multiple rounds of edits. Are you both going to do your fair share? If things get tough, is this the kind of person you feel you can have straightforward conversations with? Will you be able to constructively map out solutions together? Sometimes, sadly, the answer will be no.

And sometimes things will start out great and then go downhill. You know that egotistical-jerk host I mentioned earlier? None of his three co-hosts had any idea what a complete bully he would become with each of them. He started off acting like he enjoyed their company. Similar story with some friends I know who've co-hosted: Initially they loved working together, but eventually the stressful parts of making a show brought out the worst in them.

So what do you do if you find you and your co-host just aren't working well together, despite all your best efforts?

Honestly, my friends, I think you should just quit.

Of course, breaking up with a co-host sucks. It's like quitting a job and breaking up with a dream all at once. But consider this:

1. You know how kids always know if their mom and dad (or dad and dad, or mom and mom) are fighting? Well, listeners also know, even if you're trying your darndest to sound jolly. I know this from personal experience. You know that abusive host I keep mentioning? Well, I was one of his regular guests, and sometimes, when I was in segments with him, he'd speak to me in such a condescending tone that—even when I tried my best to meet his vitriol with humor and "yes, and" energy—listeners would write in asking why he was so mad at me.

2. If you entered into the co-hosting relationship as friends, remember how rare and wonderful a true friendship is. There are a million other people on the planet you can co-host with. How many people can you call in the middle of the night because you just had the best date ever or the worst day at work?

3. If a show isn't fun to make anymore, it's likely going to die anyway. The only thing that keeps most podcasts going is the

love for the show that the host or hosts hold for it. So don't let it die; wrap it up nicely so that you leave your listeners on a high note.

In short, have those tough conversations with your co-host. And if those tough conversations don't lead you to a happy way to continue working together, have the toughest conversation of all. I promise you'll feel relieved afterward.

Part 4

CAST IT

$((({\circ})))$

16

Get the Guests You Want

Friends, I'm going to tell you something here that's going to sound like a big old brag, and that's because it is: I am a first-rate guest booker, and I don't care how crazy the guest is.

Need to talk to Santa Claus for a story without actually revealing whether Santa is real or not? I'm on it.

Need a Christian lesbian mom who also happens to be a Boy Scout troop leader at a time when the Boy Scouts are claiming they can't have gay adults associated with their organization because they aren't "good Christians"? I've got you covered.

Need a handful of celebrities from different parts of the United States to talk about why each of them comes from the greatest music city in America? I'm here to help.

The fact is, I've booked all the above guests in less than three days' turnaround time: an accomplished Santa from a school that trains Santas; a Midwestern Christian lesbian mom who proudly leads her son's troop; and musicians ranging from Mary Wilson (of the Supremes, from Detroit) to Wayne Coyne (of the Flaming Lips, from

Oklahoma City) to Reggie Watts (Brooklyn transplant), to showcase their hometown pride.

People sometimes ask me how I got so good at booking guests. The short answer is that I love doing it. I love the detective work of finding the right people. I love being on a scavenger hunt where the big prize is an exceptional story. I love the chase.

But beyond my love for the task, there's a much more tangible secret behind all my booking acumen: I'm a first-rate pest. And by that I mean:

1. I'll find all the ways I can to track down a person and then pester them (or their associates) until I'm bordering on irritating.
2. I pester lots of people. For every one slot I want to fill, I usually reach out to at least ten potential leads.

But wait! I'm getting ahead of myself! What if you don't even know who to pester or how?

It all begins with knowing the story you want to tell. In the case of the Santa, I was putting together a series on unusual holiday-related stories, so I began doing mad research online to find stories that weren't being widely told. In the case of the lesbian Boy Scout troop leader, I was working on one of the main stories of the day, and I knew I wanted to approach it in a way that the other outlets weren't—ideally, a more human way. And in the case of the musicians and the cities, I'd been looking for a way to engage with listeners in other parts of the country—I decided on a "virtual road trip" with a soundtrack for each city, and a famous local guide.

All of the above bookings were made when I worked for a daily news radio show as the culture producer, and because culture is a giant, expansive thing, the stories I worked on varied wildly. In the case of your podcast, I'm guessing things are a little more focused. (I hope they are!)

But back to the question of how to nail down your guests. I'm going to lay out tips here for each of the main categories of people you'll likely be looking for—real people, experts, and celebrities.

Real People

In the industry, when we say "real people," we mean the humans who are being affected by a story or who are at the center of a story (such as the Christian lesbian Boy Scout troop leader). Real people are sometimes referred to as the stuff of "fluffy human interest stories"—especially in pieces like the one I produced about the Santa school. I see it differently. I think real people bring context to stories that are hard to wrap our heads around, reflect how government policies and world events are affecting individuals, and shine a spotlight on what makes us human. For the most part, we are all real people. But despite being everywhere, real people are sometimes the hardest guests to book. These are some ways to track them down:

1. Friends and family and former colleagues. A lot of journalists find sources by word of mouth, and I, personally, have found some great guests this way—by posting on my social media sites, making phone calls to friends who I know are well connected in certain communities, and asking for help from specific networking and social groups I'm involved with. But a warning: With this method, there is a risk of finding guests who have more in common with you and your friends than with your story. The sad fact is that most people's circles aren't as diverse as they think they are—in terms of geography, race, class, educational attainment, religion, political leanings, and so on. So don't make this your main way of doing things.

2. Google the words you're afraid to Google. I already said this in the diversity chapter, and I'll say it again: Everything you want is there if you just type the words. That includes "lesbian" and "Christian" and all the other words that might make you feel like you're profiling and pigeonholing people. Google the words knowing that—in doing so—you'll actually allow certain people to be seen and heard. Google them knowing they'll help your story. Google them, and I assure you: You'll find social organizations, churches, activist groups, mommy blogs, and other sources you'll need to do your best work.

3. Email and call and email some more. That means sending notes to people's private email addresses, work email addresses, LinkedIn pages, Facebook pages, and organizational "contact me" forms. It means calling them, and in some cases, calling other people who can help you track them down. It means Tweeting privately, and then, if that doesn't work, Tweeting them publicly. I'm not saying to be a stalker here, I'm saying that sometimes the first and second ways of contacting will go unnoticed, end up in spam, or just be ignored. So be persistent. (Of course, also be friendly and professional and make clear what your potential guest will get out of appearing on your show—whether it's broadening their audience, or just being able to tell their own story in their own words—but persistence is really key!)

Experts

Experts fall somewhere between "real people" and "celebrities." Some experts are famous. Some are just regular folks who walk around in the world alongside us but are hugely respected in their particular fields. Do some sleuthing online to find out which category your expert falls into. If your expert falls more into the celebrity category, jump ahead to the Celebrities section. If not, continue here:

1. If you know the specific expert you want, and the expert is associated with a university, museum, government office, company, or organization, you're in luck. That means that the contact information will be published online or easy to find with a few phone calls. Write to them directly. Call their offices. And then, if you don't hear back, reach out to the PR office at their institution.

2. If you know the expert you want and the expert is not associated with an organization, begin the task of Googling. They likely have a personal web page, a company web page, a Twitter handle, an Instagram page, and other ways that they can be contacted directly.

3. If you don't know the specific expert you want but know more broadly that you want an astronaut or physicist or teacher, Google the words. You'll likely find clubs, professional networking groups, and so on for each profession. Then email and call and email some more.

Celebrities

Celebrities are obviously famous people, and sometimes they're less obviously famous. For example, we all know movie stars and Grammy-winning musicians are famous, but in some cases, people with Instagram feeds and YouTube channels are also celebrities in their own right. When you're dealing with celebrities, prepare yourself to hear "no" a lot. And if they say yes, prepare for them to cancel. Famous people receive a lot of press requests, and sometimes you can get one to say yes, only to have them cancel on you later for a more high-profile interview opportunity. But, despite all the headaches, it can be done! I've booked Taylor Swift in less than a week and Olympic gold medalists in just a day! Here's how to do it:

1. Most big celebrities are repped by the same handful of giant agencies: CAA, WME, UTA, Paradigm, and so on. Do some Googling to find out which agency represents the celebrity you're trying to track down.

2. Call the agency. A receptionist will say, "CAA Los Angeles," and you'll reply by saying, "I'm a journalist trying to get in contact with so-and-so's agent." The receptionist will forward your call to that agent's assistant. You'll then tell the assistant, "Hi, I'm a journalist trying to get in touch with the publicist of so-and-so." The agent's assistant will give you the name and email address of the publicist you're looking for.

3. Email the publicist. Send them a note that briefly and persuasively makes clear why it would be beneficial for their very famous client to appear on your podcast (see page 91 for tips).

4. For celebrities that have recently written books, appeared in movies, or released an album, it's likely that they're already on a press tour and giving lots of interviews. If this is the case, reach out directly to the PR department of the book publisher, film studio, or record label and make clear that your intent is

to interview them about their new project (even if you plan on throwing in a few questions *not* related to that project).

5. Some celebrities are also philanthropists. If you want to talk about a charity that they're the goodwill ambassador for, or discuss the latest work that they're on the ground doing, this is sometimes the easiest ask. Reach out to their organization's PR team and make clear that you want to depict them in a good light.

How to Write a Good Pitch Email to Potential Guests

- In the subject line, write "Interview Request" and then just a bit more. (For example: "Interview Request for Carly Martinez from a Women's Government Podcast.")

- In the body of the email, introduce yourself and your show. ("Dear Ms. Martinez, My name is Marcia Washington and I'm the host of a podcast called Women of Tomorrow. In each episode I talk with a different woman who is running for public office.")

- Explain why you want to interview the person you're reaching out to. ("With your steadfast focus on education for first-generation Americans, I think you'd be a perfect guest for our show. Many of my listeners have specifically asked to hear from candidates running on education platforms.")

- Let them know when you want them, how long the interview would take, and what the connection method would be. ("I would be so honored if I could interview you sometime in the final two weeks of March, between 11 A.M. and 3 P.M. EST—it will only take about 15 minutes and can be done via Skype.") Note the importance of the time zone, as your guests may be anywhere!

- Make clear how they can get in touch with you. ("Please let me know if you'd be able to fit this into your schedule by responding to this email or phoning me at 555-123-4567. I certainly hope you can.")

- In your signature, include a bit more about your show and its prior guests, as well as links to your website and social media feeds.

- Be polite! If you're not saying "please" and "thank you" and saying something nice about them, you're doing it wrong.

- Keep it brief! Get to the point. If it's more than a dozen sentences, it's too long.

- Here's how your completed letter should look:

Subject line: Interview Request for Carly Martinez from a Women's Government Podcast.

Dear Ms. Martinez,

My name is Marcia Washington and I'm the host of a podcast called Women of Tomorrow. In each episode, I talk with a different woman who is running for public office.

With your steadfast focus on education for first-generation Americans, I think you'd be a perfect guest for our show. Many of my listeners have specifically asked to hear from candidates running on education platforms.

I would be so honored if I could interview you sometime in the final two weeks of March, between 11 A.M. and 3 P.M. EST—it will only take about 15 minutes and can be done via Skype.

Please let me know if you'd be able to fit this into your schedule by responding to this email or phoning me at 555-123-4567. I certainly hope you can.

Thank you for your time and consideration.

Sincerely,
Marcia Washington

Host, Women of Tomorrow
Phone: 555-123-4567
Twitter / Instagram / Facebook
www.showwebsiteexample.com

Women of Tomorrow is a podcast about women running for public office. Our guests have included Jenny Nguyen, Sherry Patel, and Crystal Wilson. In the past year, Women of Tomorrow has been downloaded over 10,000 times.

17

Prepare Your Guests and Yourself
for the Show

Congratulations! The guest you reached out to has responded to your interview request asking to know more. Now what?

There are a couple of ways you can go here.

First option: Seal the deal. In some cases, you'll know you want the person no matter what. You'll know they're a great talker from hearing them on other shows or watching videos of them on YouTube. You'll know you love them and won't want to waste their time and just want to get things set in stone. In those cases, write back immediately. Say thank you. Nail down an exact time for the interview. Tell them where to go (if they will be required to go to a studio, for example) or how they will be connected (Skype, phone, or other method). Reiterate how long it will take and how excited you are for the interview. Thank them again.

Second option: Pre-interview the guest. If you want to know more about your guest, set up a time to do a pre-interview by phone. A pre-interview is a brief conversation that touches on some of the topics that will be covered in the interview. It allows you to suss out if your potential guest is the best person for your story, if their experience speaks to what you want to convey, and if they are able to tell their own story in a compelling way. Warning: While everyone in the world has a great story, some people just aren't great at telling their great stories.

But how do you conduct a pre-interview? What should you say and what should you look for?

1. Explain your show, including not just the subject matter, but also the tone of your podcast. If you have a show that talks about serious issues with a light touch, make that clear. If your show is silly and absurd, relay that in your explanation. Your guest should know what they're in for and have the chance to try to bring you not just the desired content but also the desired context.

2. Make clear that you're not taping the pre-interview, but just asking a few questions to get to know the guest better.

3. Keep it brief, ideally ten minutes or less. I know I already said this, but it can sometimes be hard to do. In my early days, I sometimes so enjoyed pre-interviewing a guest that I accidentally stayed on the line with them for way longer than a real interview would last.

4. Don't read off every question you want to ask. Remember, the pre-interview is just a chance to take a closer look at your guest—it's not supposed to replicate what you'll do later. And if you let them know all the questions you want to ask, there won't be any magic during the actual sit-down interview

later. (Of course, there are some people who will insist that you go over every potential question with them in the pre-interview; these are people who hate being surprised and aren't thinking about how stiff they'll sound if they know all the questions. My advice: Just walk them through your five main bullet points instead, and make clear that you'll want the interview to sound like a conversation. In all my years, I've never pre-interviewed a guest who wasn't okay with this.)

5. Listen to what they say and take notes. Does their experience fit in with what you want to cover on your show? Are they willing to tell their story in detail?

6. Pay attention to their energy level. If they are bored, boring, or distracted during the pre-interview, don't count on them to suddenly turn it on and become the life of the party on your show.

If the pre-interview goes well, you can seal the deal on the phone, and then also follow up with a confirmation email, giving your guest all the relevant details for the interview day.

If the pre-interview goes badly, cut the conversation short and thank them for their time. Then, within twenty-four hours, send them an email thanking them once more and apologizing because you've decided to go in a different direction with your story. If you're like me, it will feel lousy the first few times you send this kind of email, but I promise it will get easier! Remember, if you know the interview won't be what you need, you are doing them a favor by not wasting more of their time. Hopefully this will happen less frequently as you get more in tune with what kinds of people you want on your show.

How to Write a Confirmation Email

- In the subject line, write "Confirmation" and then specifics about the show and interview time. (For example: "Confirmation: Interview with The Dogwalker's Club podcast, June 2, 11 A.M. EST.")

- In the body of the email, thank the guest for the pre-interview if they gave you one and express excitement about them appearing on your show. ("Dear Doug, Thank you so much for taking the time to talk with me just now about your experience walking celebrity dogs. I'm so excited to have you on The Dogwalker's Club podcast next week.")

- Remind them of the time of the interview, how long it will take, and the connection method. ("Reminder: The interview will take place at 11 A.M. EST on June 2. It will take place at the XYZ Studio at 123 Sesame Street and last about 25 minutes.")

- Let them know they can reach out to you with questions. ("If you have any questions before the interview, please don't hesitate to write or call me at 555-123-4567.")

- Thank them again, and show enthusiasm ("Thank you again! So looking forward to next Tuesday!")

- As with your pitch email, in your signature, include a bit more about your show and its prior guests, as well as links to your website and social media feeds.

Here's how your completed letter should look:

Subject line: Confirmation: Interview with The Dog-walker's Club podcast, June 2, 11 A.M. EST

Dear Doug,

Thank you so much for taking the time to talk with me just now about your experience walking celebrity dogs. I'm so excited to have you on The Dogwalker's Club podcast next week.

Reminder: The interview will take place at 11 A.M. EST on June 2. It will take place at the XYZ Studio at 123 Sesame Street and last about 25 minutes.

If you have any questions before the interview, please don't hesitate to write or call me at 555-123-4567.

Thank you again! So looking forward to next Tuesday!

Sincerely,
Tamika Walker
Host, The Dogwalker's Club
Phone: 555-123-4567
Twitter / Instagram / Facebook
www.showwebsiteexample.com

The Dogwalker's Club is a podcast hosted by five-time Cincinnati Dogwalker of the Year Tamika Walker. In each episode, Tamika talks with people who make their living walking dogs—or just love taking a stroll with their canines.

18

Conduct a First-Rate Interview

Interviews can be scary, at least at first. You want to ask your questions, but you don't want to sound like you're reading them. You want to sound conversational, but not so conversational that you're going off on a million tangents. You want to showcase the best or most interesting aspects of your guests, and you also want to bring out something unexpected in each one. It's a lot to mentally keep track of.

Some people just have a natural knack for leading great interviews. I'm thinking of a host I worked with a few years ago named Sam Zabell. Sam was just out of college, working for *Real Simple,* and hosting the magazine's podcast called Adulthood Made Easy. In each episode, Sam talked with different guests about topics ranging from job interviews to student loan debt to dealing with lousy roommates to attending high school reunions. And regardless of who she sat down with—from best-selling authors to celebrities to investment bankers to young people living on their own for the first time—she always sounded truly interested, and the guests sounded truly interesting.

Incredibly, Sam never read her questions off a script. She had a couple points jotted down but rarely looked at them. Instead, she just had conversations. She was and is the most natural interviewer I've ever met. I was in total awe of her then and I'm still in awe of her today.

Now, gentle readers, I don't expect you to sit down at a mic with a complete stranger and be the next Sam Zabell right off the bat. But I know for sure you have the main ingredient Sam always attributed her interviewing magic to: curiosity. Like Sam, you are interested in people and their stories. You enjoy learning about others. You think the world is made better every time two people connect. If you didn't think so, you wouldn't be going through all the effort to interview them.

And on top of that, you're a great host. I know this because you've already read the hosting chapters.

All that being said, there are some concrete things you can do to make things easier on you and your guests. Specifically:

1. Be prepared. Learn what you can about your guest in advance. Familiarize yourself with their work, their passions, their accomplishments, their setbacks, where they grew up, and what they're aiming to do next. Read something they've written, watch a movie they've starred in, or listen to other interviews they've given. Know not just *about* them, but know for certain *why* you want to talk with them. Doing so will help you feel more confident going in and more at ease during the conversation.

2. Know the five most important questions you want answered or the five main points you want to hit. Very likely, you'll have way more than five questions, but there's a chance that, if things are going well and the conversation is flowing, you won't get to all of them. So know the five main plot points of your conversation and be sure to hit those.

3. Make your guest feel welcome. Thank them for their time. Let them know how happy you are to be talking with them. Give them the general tone of things. ("This is going to be a light, frothy conversation about your first job.") Remind them how long you'll be talking. Let them know that everything is being taped, not live, and that they can always restate things or correct themselves during the conversation.

4. Start with questions that make them feel at ease. Don't head out of the gates asking, "Why did you embezzle that money from the ice cream store you managed?" Talk first about the backstory, the ice cream, the work.

5. Do more listening than talking. Of course, we already know you do this, because you're curious. But some hosts really have a hard time with listening. One host I worked with was so adamant about bringing his own opinion and story to the table that the majority of his interviews were dominated by his voice rather than the guests'. Don't be like that host. Don't make every interview about you. Let your guests talk. And listen closely to what they're saying.

6. Ask follow-up questions. When your guest tells you something interesting, don't just move on to the next question on your list. Ask a follow-up question. Be human. Let them be human. See where things take you. Eventually you'll be able to circle back to the five main points you want to hit.

7. Push the right people on the hard questions. Have you heard the term "softball question"? In journalism terms, it's the opposite of a hard-hitting question. And when you're

interviewing politicians or CEOs or other public figures who run the world, softballs should be few and far between. They make you look like an amateur, they deprive your audience of something truly interesting, and they imply that you don't care about the truth. For example, a few years back a late-show host was interviewing a candidate running for public office who had been caught on tape bragging about assaulting women. But during the interview, the host focused on the politician's hair care routine and other light subjects, rather than address the elephant in the room. Not only was the host pilloried by the press, but the interview was a complete bore.

8. Bring out the humanity in others. Scholars (see p. 132), celebrities, and everyday people should not—for the most part—be handled the same way as politicians. To crib from a popular magazine: Listeners, more than anything, want to know how these people are "just like us." What insecurities do they have? What mistakes have they made? Who was their favorite teacher? What did they love most about growing up in Kansas? Get on the same page as them, let them know they're safe to share these stories, laugh with them when it's appropriate, and show empathy where it's warranted.

9. More than anything, be you.

What to Do After the Interview

First and foremost, thank them. Tell them you appreciate them and their time. Next, send them an email:

1. thanking them again for their time. (No, this isn't redundant! You can't say thank you too many times!);

2. telling them that you'll send a link to the episode they appeared in when it's published and out in the world.

When the episode is ready, follow through and send the link. The guest will appreciate it, and if you ask, they may even post it to their social media sites and promote it in other ways.

19

Consider Getting a Producer

I love my producers. I *love love love* them. They work their tails off to make me sound good. They tell me when I'm going off on a tangent or slurring my words. They cut out the stuff that makes me sound like an idiot. They are truly superheroes.

Cameron Drews, Lindsey Kratochwill, Nora Ritchie, I'm talking to you three.

But I don't just love my producers. I have a lot of empathy for them. Their work is hard and often thankless. While hosts get all the accolades, producers are often forgotten. I know this because I used to be a producer. I've produced over a dozen shows in my life—at one point, I was producing more than half a dozen at the same time—and while some hosts went out of their way to show me that they valued my input and thank me out loud in every episode, there were certainly those who didn't.

So first things first, I want to warn you: Show the utmost appreciation for your producers, or deal with the fact that I'll be very, very disappointed in you.

Okay, now that we have that out of the way, let's deal with the big question most new podcasters have: What exactly does a producer do?

The short answer is: everything but host (though sometimes, a producer is a stand-in host, as well).

Here are the main things I've done as a producer, and that my producers have done for me:

- create production schedules
- generate original story ideas
- book and pre-interview unique guests
- write well-researched scripts in the voices of the hosts
- connect remote guests to the hosts
- greet and set up in-person guests
- oversee the technical aspects of recording episodes
- direct hosts during recording sessions
- edit episodes focusing on story, continuity, and sound design
- note issues with first cuts of episodes and oversee pickup recording sessions in which corrections are made
- do second (and sometimes third and fourth and fifth) edits of episodes
- write episode descriptions and titles that are compelling enough for people to click on
- publish episodes via hosting and distribution platforms
- keep track of ad copy and ad schedules
- produce compelling advertisements that meet advertiser guidelines
- promote episodes via social media
- arrange for hosts to be guests on other shows
- design web pages that include the episodes, press, bios, and so on
- interact with listeners on social media
- produce live shows

Of course, producers do way more than this! They also help keep everyone calm, give constructive feedback, send lots of emails and thank you notes, lead a variety of meetings, head up location scouts, capture sound from the field, and sometimes even manage budgets.

I love being an audio producer. It's fun. It's creative. There are always a variety of tasks to do. And I love interacting with all the people involved in the podcast.

But it's also incredibly hard, and I'm not just talking about the fact that some hosts take you for granted. It's challenging to juggle all that work and do it well. Some parts of the job are downright tedious (for each producer, those parts are different).

If you're just starting out, you may already know the work that goes into being a producer—because you're already doing it, on your own. This was certainly the case with me. When I was co-hosting my first podcast, Movie Date, with Rafer Guzman, I was the producer as well. And, for the most part, I loved being both producer and host. I liked feeling like I was involved with every part of the show. I liked booking the guests and cutting out all the parts of our conversations where I sounded lousy.

Rafer certainly appreciated my work and told me so constantly, but he also expressed multiple times his desire for a producer who wasn't me. "Imagine how great it would be if you could just concentrate on hosting while someone else did the dirty work?" By dirty work, Rafer meant stepping in when we were going off on tangents, helping us to stick to our structure, and editing the show with the confidence and freedom that accompany the task when it's not your own voice on tape.

The fact is, we couldn't afford a producer. We'd occasionally had interns help us with the editing, but not the directing or booking of guests or other tasks. And because they weren't a part of the entire process, they could never fully do the job to the best of their abilities. And a tiny part of me was fine with that. I wasn't fully ready to have the show taken away from my controlling grasp.

In hindsight, though, I agree with Rafer 100 percent. We should have had a separate producer. The show was good. We had funny segments and famous guests, and more than anything, we had great on-air chemistry. But the show would have been so much better if we'd had someone else bossing us around and fixing our mistakes.

I came to this realization less than a year after Movie Date ended, when Jolenta and I were working on developing By the Book at Panoply as part of their "Panoply Pilot Project." The project was actually a contest. Panoply selected four podcast ideas to develop into pilot episodes, the public would then vote on their favorite episodes, and the winners would eventually be green-lit and turned into full seasons.

There was a lot of buzz around the project, and obviously, Panoply wanted all the pilots to be outstanding. And so they didn't just tell the four show makers to develop their podcasts with occasional feedback from the higher-ups; they assigned each of us a producer. Ours was the great Cameron Drews. Additionally, the outstanding Mia Lobel and Laura Mayer served as managing producer and executive producer, respectively, on all the pilots.

The experience of working with a real production team was life-changing. Cameron's ears were focused on everything from the differences between how Jolenta and I talked into the mics (not always easy to notice if you're hosting and directing at the same time) to inconsistencies with our story lines. Meanwhile, Mia and Laura were addressing structural issues from day one, and thinking constantly about the first five minutes of the show (see Chapter 7: Create a Structure and Chapter 8: Focus on the Top for more on this).

The thing is, even the most experienced podcast host/producer (I'm referring to myself here) can benefit enormously from outside ears. All those talented people in the room with Jolenta and me heard more than we heard, and they heard it all without their egos and biases in the way.

So here's my recommendation:

Cast It

1. Learn all you can about the production process. Being a producer made me a better host. And being a host made me a
   better producer. Knowing all the parts of the machine means
   you can fix any part of the machine, and it also means you
   can prevent certain problems from happening in the first
   place. For example, if you have to edit out a million "um"s
   and "uh"s when you're producing, then you're less likely to
   say all those "um"s and "uh"s the next time you're hosting.
   And if the scripts you're reading into the mic as a host sound
   clunky, you'll start writing them better when you put your
   producer hat back on.

2. After that, get a producer if you can afford one. They're
   listed on sites like AIR (Association of Independents in
   Radio), audio listservs, Facebook podcasting communities,
   college media departments, and elsewhere. Some producers
   specialize in booking guests and writing scripts but not in
   the technical stuff like connecting guests and running the
   boards. Some are outstanding sound designers, but maybe
   your show doesn't need all the bells and whistles. My recommendation is to know what tasks you need help with and
   have your producer work with you on just a few episodes to
   see if they can do those things well. And if there're only one
   or two tasks they can help with, let them be editing, because
   that's the most time-consuming, and directing your recording sessions—because having someone tell you the truth in
   studio will make everything about your show better.

3. But if you can't afford a producer (and even if you can), be
   sure to get outside feedback on your show—and not just
   from your co-host. For more on this step, move on to the next
   chapter!

A Maker v. A Manager

"I'm a maker, not a manager!"

I used to say this a lot in the days before I had producers. I said it because I wanted to have my hands in all the pots. I said it because I was a control freak. Above all, I said it because I wanted to be creative in all the ways there were to be creative. I did not see managing as creative. And then I met the great Sam Dingman, host and creator of Family Ghosts. Sam loves managing and he also happens to be great at it, and if it weren't for his encouragement, I probably would never have said yes to being a manager myself. His magic words (paraphrased): "Building and managing a team is a creative act. It's not simply about logistics, it's about finding ways to inspire each person on your team to do their best work, and figuring out how to get very different people to work together in inventive ways. And when you work together, you and your team will flex creative muscles you never realized you had on your own." Sam was right: Managing is another way of making, and everything that goes into making a show is, in fact, creative.

20

Turn to the Right People for Feedback

Friends, I've dated a lot of musicians and a few artists and a handful of stand-up comics over the course of my life, and I have to tell you: More often than not, it was not fun giving them feedback. It was not fun watching their bands play mediocre rip-offs of Norwegian death metal songs. It was disappointing to know that I locked lips with people who made art so horrible I'd be embarrassed to hang it in a doghouse. It was exhausting to listen to unfunny men pour all their hearts into being funny when I couldn't imagine who in the world would pay to hear them tell jokes.

In most cases, I would try to love them separately from their art. But it wasn't easy. Sometimes I'd get dragged in. Sometimes I would try to be a good girlfriend and go to their concert or art opening or comedy night or interactive talking-object showcase. And afterward, they'd always ask, "What did you think?"

How do you give feedback to someone you like as a person but don't really enjoy creatively? More often than not, with empty words like: "You did it!" or "I love that you're living your dream!" or "I'm so proud of you" or "You are the absolute best."

I know, I know. Those kinds of hollow compliments aren't constructive and they don't help the creative person in your life get better, but I honestly believe this is what's to be expected when you ask the people you share your heart with to give you feedback on your special projects.

And that's why I have one big rule when it comes to asking for feedback: Don't try to solicit it from people who love you. That means your kids, your mom, your significant other—all of them. Don't ask them to read scripts. Don't beg them to come to a live taping. And for the love of Pete, don't ask them to sit there and listen to one of your podcasts while you stare at them, smiling and nodding desperately.

Please just leave them out of this.

Now, at this point, it would be totally acceptable for you to say, "But hold on! Isn't your husband actually in every episode of By the Book? How can you say not to involve your loved ones, but then do it yourself?"

Here's how: because even though he's in the show, my beloved husband, Dean, does not actually listen to the show. He claims that he listened to a few episodes in the first season, just to be supportive, but honestly, I don't think he even did that.

The fact is, I don't want Dean to listen. When we first started dating, I came right out and told him, "Your job is not to listen to the shows I host, guest-host, give interviews to, or produce. You already have a job, and it has nothing to do with audio. And you have a hobby, which is making out with me. I don't want you to be a fan, and for crying out loud, I don't want you to be the opposite of a fan. I just want you to be my boyfriend."

All right, now that that's out of the way, let's get to the real issue here: If you shouldn't ask your loved ones for feedback on your podcast, who should you ask?

To start with, *ask yourself.* After the episode is edited and put out into the world, listen to it closely, minute by minute, and take notes. At three minutes in, did the energy drop? Note it. At minute seven, did it seem that the story you started at minute five had already gone on way too long? Write it down. And don't just note what's falling short; pay attention to what's really working.

If you have a co-host and/or producer and/or other contributors, make close listening an assignment for everyone on your team. Listen separately, all on your own time, noting what makes you cringe, what feels clunky and sloppy, and what makes you laugh or feel something deeply. Afterward, email your notes to each other and talk about how you can improve going forward. Repeat when the next episode drops, and the next episode after that.

Ask your listeners. Say to them in each episode that you want their feedback. Ask them to tell you what they want more of or less of. Are there stories they wish you would cover that you're not? Are there guests they would love for you to bring on? Give them a way to reach out to you and tell you.

Join a podcast club. They exist in a lot of cities, or you can start one of your own. In a podcast club, aspiring podcast makers share their work, give each other tips, and receive feedback on their works in progress. As with all clubs, you'll be expected not just to bask in all the feedback, but give it to others—a task that I promise will also make you a better podcaster.

Take a class. There are audio-production classes available at reasonable prices at community centers, arts organizations, and schools. If you have the money, take a class—not just to hone your craft but because you'll have a built-in circle of teachers and fellow students to seek feedback from and give feedback to.

Should Your Dream Team Include a Lawyer?

Most up-and-coming podcasters feel their bases are covered with a co-host, producer, guests, and some trusted people to give them feedback. But others feel they need one more person to get the ball rolling: a lawyer. After all, a lawyer knows a lot more about intellectual property—whether related to one's ownership of a show title, or the components that go into making a show (like music, which we'll talk more about in Part 5, "Make It"). Lawyers also come in handy if you ever want to bring a show to a network or take a show out of a network (which we'll discuss more in Part 6, "Share It"). They're also worth consulting if you're covering territory that has the potential to get sticky, like a true-crime story. I, myself, have talked with a lawyer in the past, as have many of my podcasting friends, and we're better for the experience.

If you're inclined to hire a lawyer but aren't sure where to begin, ask others in the podcasting sphere for referrals, and then talk to a few. Many lawyers offer free initial consultations, which give you the chance to figure out if they're the right fit for you and your needs. And bonus: If a friend refers you, many lawyers will charge you a lower rate.

Part 5

MAKE IT

$$(((\circ)))$$

21

Know the Equipment You'll Actually Need

Before we jump into this chapter, I just want to remind you of something I said at the very beginning of this book: This is not a technical guide. Yes, I'm going to mention a few brand names, but I'm not going to advocate for any of them. Yes, I'm going to tell you what I think you need, but I'm not going to tell you step-by-step how to use every piece of equipment. For gadget and software training, I highly recommend talking to real people in real life, or watching videos that show rather than tell you what to do.

Now that that's out of the way, I'm going to tell you something that no tech retailer, gadget review site, or gearhead wants you to know: Most of the stuff out there being peddled to aspiring podcasters is not necessary to make a good show.

As I see it, you really need only a few pieces of equipment (in addition to your computer) to make a great-sounding podcast:

1. A decent microphone (two if you have a co-host, three if you're interviewing guests). And yes, I said decent. Not top-of-the-line, not expensive. *Decent.* That's because when you

hit a certain quality level in microphones, the differences between them are minuscule. So don't break the bank on your microphone. Get one that's decent. And get one that you're not afraid of. For beginners, that often means USB microphones that can be plugged directly into your computer, along with a pop shield (a little screen that attaches to the microphone to cut down on popping sounds).

2. Headphones. You'll want to know how you sound as you're talking into the mic, and just listening to your own voice without headphones won't suffice. Without headphones, you won't know when you've wandered too far from the mic or hit the mic with your hand or are shaking the table. You'll also want headphones while you edit, to help you listen more closely to all the sounds you'll be working on—including breaths that you might not hear otherwise.

3. Recording and editing software. Adobe Audition, Garage-Band, and Audacity are all popular choices for new podcasters. I personally like to edit in Hindenburg. In the past, I've used DAVID. My friends in the industry mostly prefer Pro Tools. There are no right or wrong answers here, but I do urge you to start out with something that's not too intimidating or expensive.

4. A portable audio recorder (optional). A portable XLR recorder allows you to record anywhere on multiple tracks in high quality. That means that if you have two or three microphones, each microphone you plug in will be recorded as a separate audio file. These devices require XLR microphones (as opposed to the USB microphones mentioned above) and a memory card (the machine will record all the tracks onto a

memory card that you can then easily transfer to your computer), as well as lots of AA batteries. Popular brand names include Zoom, Marantz, and Panasonic. I love portable XLR recorders, but warning: They can be pricey—anywhere from $100 to $500 when you buy them brand-new.

On top of all this, you'll need something that I consider of the utmost importance: a quiet room. That's because even the best mic, recording equipment, and editing software can't disguise a loud or echo-y recording space.

Of course, you know what causes a loud room: street noises, your neighbors, planes flying overhead, traffic, wild animals, the dishwasher, other members of your household, and so on.

What's less understood is the cause of that tin-can sound that so many podcasts suffer from. Many podcasters mistakenly presume it's due to a substandard mic. Others blame it on faulty recording equipment. But in fact, that echo-y sound is almost always caused by their own voices bouncing off hard surfaces. Those surfaces include walls, floors, ceilings, windows, desks, tables, and their own computer monitors.

Once they realize this, some podcasters try to cut down on the echoes by purchasing hundreds of square feet of expensive acoustic panels (those padded things you'll sometimes see on the walls of a music store). Or maybe they'll try to move their whole operation to a studio.

Personally, I love recording in a studio. Studios sound great. They have all the acoustic panels on the walls already. And there are always people there to help you. But a lot of folks starting out can't afford studios. In some cases, they cost over $200 per hour.

And in my opinion, most of us already have a studio-quality room in our homes: a closet. Closets have all the acoustic padding you'll need, in the form of the clothes hanging up. Closets block out background noise because they're normally not windowed or facing the street. And bonus—they're free of distractions!

But hold on—what if you have a co-host? Or a guest? Will a closet really work? Or what if your closets are all super-tiny?

In that case, I suggest you try a small room with soft surfaces. So instead of a kitchen, for example, try recording in a small bedroom with draperies and lots of blankets and rugs (and be sure to hang some comforters over the closets and doors). If you have a small carpeted den, try that. The furniture, books, and carpet will help absorb the sound (and again, try that comforter trick).

And don't worry if your setup doesn't look as pretty or polished as a professional studio. I've given interviews in bedrooms, dens, and closets. In the end, all I really cared about was that I sounded good, and that's all you should care about too.

22

Connect with Your Guests

Earlier, in Chapter 16, you may have noticed that our guest-booking letters included lines like "The interview will take place at XYZ Studio" or "The interview can be done via Skype."

Now, in my perfect world, all interviews would be done face-to-face in Oprah's original Harpo Productions studios. But sadly, I don't know Oprah, and those Chicago studios haven't existed in years.

So let me walk you through all the other methods you can use to connect with your guests, as well as the benefits and drawbacks of each method:

1. Have the guest come to your home studio. The benefits: It's your home base, where you have an established setup. And when you and your guest are both there, you don't have to deal with potentially faulty connection methods. The drawbacks: If your guest lives far away, this won't work. And even if your guest lives nearby, they may not want to go to a place that feels like a less-than-legit operation. As I said in the last

chapter, a lot of guests (myself included) don't care. But the more high-profile ones may prefer another option.

2. Rent a recording studio that you can both go to. When you rent a recording studio, you get a quiet room, the fancy microphones and headphones, the audio files themselves, and usually a staff engineer who will oversee the recording. The benefits: The experience will feel professional for your guest, you won't have to worry about technical stuff during the interview, and you will come away with a recording that has outstanding sound quality. The drawbacks: Studio costs can add up quickly, and this only works if both you and your guest are within a reasonable distance of each other.

3. Go to them with your portable recorder, microphones, and headsets. You know the XLR portable recorder I mentioned in the last chapter? It's the equivalent of a recording studio that you can carry in your hands. You can bring it anywhere. The benefits: Your guest doesn't have to travel, and you should be able to come away with a great-sounding recording. The drawbacks: You can't control all the background noise. If you go to their home or their office, you may be competing with ringing phones, random people walking by and talking, and all the other noises that are a part of real life. And your guest may live too far away to make this viable.

4. Tape-sync done by you and your guest. I hate the term "tape-sync" because it sounds super-technical and intimidating. The fact is that a tape-sync is just a fancy-schmancy way of saying that both you and your guest will be recording on your ends, and talking to each other on the phone at the

same time. Get it? The phone call itself is not being recorded. But both ends of the conversation are being recorded by the participants. In some cases, the host sends the guest a USB microphone to plug into their computer for the interview and mail back afterward. When the interview begins, the guest just hits *record* on QuickTime or GarageBand or Sound Recorder or another program. When it's done, they stop it, save it, and email it to you so that you can edit and mix it with your own recording of yourself. The benefits: great sound quality, as long as your guest's home is fairly quiet. Also, no one has to travel. The drawbacks: Many guests aren't technically savvy enough or confident enough to do this.

5. Tape-sync with the help of a producer. Since the majority of guests are unfamiliar with recording their voices and are not podcasters themselves, the standard tape-sync method is to hire a producer who lives near the guest to go to them with a portable recorder, headset, and microphone. The host will call the guest on the phone, while the producer holds their own microphone up to the guest's mouth. The host will talk into a microphone and record their side of the conversation on their end. It's more or less the same as the above method, except the guest doesn't have to worry about the equipment or software. The benefits: great sound quality, as long as the guest's home or office is quiet. It doesn't matter where your guest lives, as there's likely a producer not too far away. The drawbacks: A producer costs money, usually $150 per hour.

6. Tape-sync in which your guest is in a studio and you're at home. This is a mix of methods two and five. You will rent a studio for your guest to go to. The engineer there will set up

your guest at a microphone and record on their end. You will connect with them by phone, while recording yourself into a microphone at the same time. The benefits: outstanding sound quality. The drawbacks: again, those studio costs.

7. Skype. Contact your guest via a Skype call and record them and yourself as you talk. Skype is not great, but more often than not, it sounds better than a phone. The benefits: Skype is easy for most people to use. The drawbacks: Guest sound quality can be hit-or-miss.

8. Phone. This is my absolute last resort for connecting to guests. Phones sound horrible on podcasts, and plenty of listeners will hit *stop* as soon as they hear a horrible-sounding phone call. So please, don't use a phone unless you absolutely have to. And if you do, please use a landline, not a cell, and please limit your time on the phone to a short interview segment. In my opinion, there's only one case when it's okay to use cell phones, and that's when you're covering news on the ground and there's no other way to reach your guests. For example, when I was producing stories on the 2010 earthquake in Haiti, cell phones were our only option, but that was (thankfully) a rare situation. The benefits: Everyone has a cell phone. The drawbacks: They sound horrible.

In addition to all the above methods, there are web and app connection methods such as ipDTL and Report-IT that can simulate a studio connection. Do your research, because each method has its benefits and drawbacks, as well as its updates and reissues, and I can't speak to all of them with confidence.

It may sound like a lot to juggle, but you can do it!

23

Be a Top-Notch Editor

Are you ready to play God? You'd better be, because it's time to make the world of sound bend to your will! Or, to put it slightly less dramatically, it's the moment when you get to sit down in front of your computer with your raw audio tracks and cut them apart and put them back together.

At this point, you should already have picked out editing software to work with. Perhaps you even used your editing software to record your podcast. During your taping, you hopefully recorded yourself, your co-host, and guests on separate tracks. That makes for smoother editing and a better final product. But if you're not all on separate tracks, that's also not the end of the world, as long as you're doing a straightforward talk show, rather than a more complex production with lots of moving parts.

Now, reminder: I told you at the beginning of this book that I wasn't going to walk you through how to use all the editing software out there. I honestly think it's much better to learn how to use software from a person (huge shout-out here to Joel Meyer, Jim Colgan, and Jay Cowit—the WNYC people who first taught me my way around editing software). Second to a person, I recommend video tutorials. I do not recommend a book—not mine (I'm not going to write one) or anyone else's.

However, I do have some tips that I think all podcasters should follow when editing their shows. Here goes:

1. Consider getting a transcript of all your raw audio to help you—particularly if you're doing a documentary-style podcast. A transcript makes it easier to find those magic moments in your tape, and can help you put together a road map of your show during the early stages of editing. You can use a digital service like Trint or pay a human.

2. Focus on story first, the bits and pieces second. A lot of new podcasters will jump into their tape and immediately search for all the coughs, "um"s, "uh"s, and weird mouth noises that they want to cut. But, when you're starting out, I'm going to urge you to put those irritating noises on the back burner and think of the big picture first. Listen through your tape and ask yourself: Out of all you recorded, what supports the story you want to tell, and what doesn't? What points are coming through loudest and clearest and what just sounds confusing and incongruous? Are there ways the tape can be rearranged to tell a better story? Ask these questions first, and cut the tape accordingly.

3. Pay attention to your heart and your gut. If something makes you feel all the feels, keep it. If it makes you laugh or cry or understand the plight of your guest better, treat it like gold. Likewise, pay attention to when your attention starts to fade and where you zone out. If something is dragging for you—

the person who's most invested in this podcast—then it will absolutely drag for the listener, as well.

4. Don't edit things in a way that twists your guests' words or takes what they say out of context. Don't turn them into people with different stories or different opinions. Do what you can to make them sound like the truest version of themselves.

5. Get rid of rambling. Sometimes when you're warming up with your co-host or building rapport with your guest, you'll find yourself talking for too long about things that have absolutely no relevance to your show or your listeners. And, even with the best of planning, you may find yourself going off on occasional tangents. Leave those ramblings on the cutting-room floor. I don't care if they were fun to record. It's essential that you trim the fat. I promise the meat will taste way more delicious when you do.

6. Delete all the irritations. That means the coughs, sneezes, sticky mouth noises, guests hitting the mic, pens tapping the table, and unexpected background noises.

7. Cut most, but not all, the "um"s and "uh"s and "like"s. Sometimes you or a guest will say "um" and "uh" and "like" so much that you will want to throw all your tape in the trash. Please don't! Do your best to edit most of those irritations out, but not all of them. Leave the ones in that blur into the next word. For example, *K*'s in "like"s frequently spill into the next word ("I was, like, up all night" will actually come across as "I was lie-cup all night"), which means when you cut that "like," you may also be cutting a microsecond off the

top of that next word. It will sound horribly unnatural. And hold on to a couple "um"s and "uh"s for those moments when you're trying to connect two phrases or sentences that don't sound completely smooth together. Dropping an "um" or "uh" in between them will make the connection sound natural.

8. Don't make abrupt edits. Don't cut in a way that messes with the natural pacing and tone of how people speak. Don't cut off a sentence partway through and try to fool listeners into thinking that's the end of the sentence. Don't try to mash together two fragments recorded with different tempos unless you want your listeners to stop in their tracks. Pay attention to where people's voices go up, down, build excitement, and soften—and then make sure that anything you try to trim, pull apart, or put back together matches how they talk.

9. Pay attention to breaths. Don't ever cut a breath halfway through, and don't ever edit two parts of a conversation together in a way that makes it sound like you or a guest is taking two unnatural breaths in a row or taking overlapping breaths.

10. Keep your volume levels solid. I'm hoping that when you recorded all your audio, you set up your mics correctly and talked into them the right way. But even then, you may end up with some pops, some loud laughs, and a couple whispers. Be sure to smooth those out. And, obviously, make sure you and your co-host and guests sound like you're speaking at the same volume by setting up your separate tracks at the same volume (if you recorded the tracks separately), or manually leveling out your combined tracks in post production (if you recorded on one track).

11. Make sure that you're using music in the correct way. Don't make it too loud. Don't have it run on too long before, during, or after the conversation. If your show starts with music, play only three to five seconds of the song to set the mood before we hear your voice. Listeners like music, but they get bored quickly, and besides, they're listening for you, not the music. And on that note, if you have a theme song, please keep it around 30 seconds or less.

12. Save, save, save. Every few minutes, make sure you're saving your edits. Editing is a lot of work, and there are few things more heartbreaking as an editor than having your whole session crash on you after four hours of cutting and trimming when you haven't saved any of your work.

And two final things that should go without saying:

In addition to all of the above, you should use your editing to help you be a better host, guest booker, and engineer. As you edit, you'll come across moments that make you cringe. You'll hear that your sound quality is lousy because you didn't set your guest up at the right distance from the mic. You'll realize that the guest you were on the fence about in the pre-interview is indeed the most monotone person on the planet. You'll wonder why you didn't ask questions more clearly or read from your script with more enthusiasm. As mentioned on page 128, you'll hear every "um," "uh," and "like." Don't ignore these moments or just cut them and forget them. Write them down and use them to help you do better the next time you're booking a guest, setting up a guest, conducting an interview, writing, or reading from the page. Eventually you'll look back on your earlier podcasts and be thrilled with how much you've learned and how far you've come.

Finally, of course, have fun. Editing is a creative process that allows you to pull all the strings in the universe of sound. It allows you to invent worlds and tell stories in a way that no other art or craft does. Enjoy that power, and use it to make something truly beautiful.

My Worst Moment of Not Saving My Work Correctly

Back in my final week of college, my mother and nanna saw me have one of the worst meltdowns of my life. I had just completed writing my senior thesis on my secondhand laptop (my first computer ever, purchased with waitressing money at a garage sale a few months earlier). As I triumphantly hit *save* on the final academic achievement of my undergraduate life, the entire screen went black. "Oh FFS," I'm sure I mouthed. Or maybe something worse. I tried to restart my computer, but of course it wouldn't restart. And then I tried again. And again. Eventually, my panic descended into silent rage. "I'm going outside and I'm smoking an entire pack of cigarettes by myself," I told my mother and nanna, both of whom detested smoking. Neither tried to stop me. A half hour later, my friend Dave showed up. I'm not sure if my mother and nanna called him to settle me down, or if Dave and I had prior plans. Either way, he was there, and the evening got better after that. Dave fiddled with my computer and eventually managed to bring back over half my paper. But I still had to write the second half all over again. I stayed up all night and wrote it, and turned it in just in time.

Now, why am I talking at length about the tragedy of my senior college thesis in a book about podcasting? Because friends, as bad as it was, failing to save podcast-editing sessions correctly has made me feel worse. *Way worse.*

That's because, while my senior-thesis fiasco affected only me, my podcasting catastrophes have affected thousands—and sometimes hundreds of thousands—of people. They've affected the loyal listeners who've gotten their content late—or even worse, gotten a messed-up version of their favorite show because I accidentally exported an almost-final rather than a final version of an episode. They've affected my hardworking colleagues whose names are also on my projects. And embarrassingly and horribly, they've affected the hosts who've put their trust in me to edit their shows in the best way I know how.

All this is to say, save your work. Save it early and often. Then check what you saved again, and save it one last time for good measure. You'll be thankful that you did.

24

Understand How to Use Music, Movie Clips, and More

Gentle readers, I really hope you're not making a music show. If you are, there's a high likelihood that in roughly three seconds you're going to throw this book in the trash, set the trash on fire, and then call me a bunch of horrible names. That's because I'm going to tell you not to do it.

You read that correctly: Don't do it. Don't plan on doing it. Don't invest any more of yourself or your heart into this idea. That's because all the songs you love—every song you know the words to, all the songs by all the Top 40 performers and Billboard Hot 100 stars and indie singer-songwriters and R&B chart-toppers—almost every single one of them is off-limits.

If you're like most aspiring music show hosts, I know what you're going to say: "But but but, what about Song Exploder or Broken Record or Hit Parade or all the other shows that talk about music history and the music industry? What about them?! They play dozens of song clips in every episode and no one is complaining!"

You know what? You're right. There are some hugely successful shows out there telling great music stories with impunity. They're doing it, and they're killing it. But I'm going to tell you a secret: In most cases, that's because these shows are housed within larger organizations—often journalism operations—with legal departments that have reviewed all the intellectual property laws and talked at length with record labels and struck deals with artists. These shows are the exception, not the rule.

I'm going to presume that you're not a large organization with a legal department. I'm going to wager that you don't have the money to pay enormous fines if you're accused of stealing music, or anything else for that matter. And I'm going to guess that it will break your heart if you're forced to take down your show because it violates intellectual property laws. I don't want your heart to be broken and I don't want your wallet to be empty. So don't do it.

But let's say, like the vast majority of podcasters, you actually have no interest in making a music show. Maybe you're rolling your eyes at this whole music show conversation and saying: "I just want to use a couple songs I love in each episode to set the mood! I just want my favorite hit by my favorite artist to be my theme song. It won't be a music show!"

Friends, I'm sorry. You can't. You don't own the music. And now you're not even talking about the music or giving credit to the artist. You're just using the music as wallpaper. Please don't. There's a small chance you'll be able to get away with it. But there's also a chance you'll be caught. And besides, do you really want to be a thief? Of course you don't.

Okay, now that I've been a complete killjoy, I'm going to offer some words of solace to you: Not *all* music is off-limits. In fact, there are tens of thousands of songs you can use that are legal, high quality, and in many cases, royalty-free. Some podcasters refer to this music as "podsafe."

In order for music to be podsafe, its licensing requirements must allow for it to be free for use in podcasts. In some cases, you'll have to do some detective work to find out if it is. In other cases it will be obvious because it will be a public domain work. Most music under Creative Commons licenses is also podsafe. But a warning: Most of this music is not stuff that you or your listeners will know. So if you're looking for your favorite Beatles or Bowie or Barbra Streisand song, you'll be out of luck.

And then there are audio libraries. These include Epidemic, Audio-Jungle, Marmoset, Warner/Chappell, and lots more. Each library has thousands of songs that vary wildly between sounding like the stock music songs they are and sounding eerily like your favorite Top 40 hit. Some libraries allow you to pay per song, some require you to have a paid membership, and some are just a free-for-all. But warning: Even with these libraries, it's worth reading the fine print and having a phone conversation with a rep.

If you want an original theme song or original compositions to be folded into your show, you can hire a composer. In most cases, you'll have to pay your composer, but on rare occasions, the composer/performer will be willing to do it for free in exchange for mentions on every episode of your show and links to their website in your show notes. Regardless of what the agreement is, and with whom, be sure to get it in writing. That way, if you break up with your boyfriend/composer (a situation that I witnessed on a fairly high-profile show) or you become so famous that your composer wants a bigger fee on your next project (which would only be fair), you have a paper trail of what's been agreed upon and a precedent for the future.

Okay, enough about music. Let's talk about a subject that I think is going to make you a lot happier: movies. The great thing about movie clips and trailers is that press teams for movie studios put them out into the world with the express purpose of them being used by the press. That's why you end up seeing the same movie clips over and over again when celebrities are giving interviews to all the entertainment shows about their new blockbuster. And that's why you see the same trailer (or hear it) on every movie YouTube channel and podcast. Feel free to use those same clips and trailers if you're going to review movies or talk at length about movies. Or, if you want to be more professional about it, reach out to the movie's press reps and ask for an EPK (electronic press kit), which will include clips, trailers, interviews, and more. You can do the same for TV shows.

That being said, remember that rule about not using your favorite music as wallpaper? The same applies to movie and TV clips: They're not there for you to put a finer point on something you're saying or add comic relief. As such, you can't just drop in a scene of Kermit and Miss Piggy to exemplify how much you love your girlfriend, or a scene of Bridget Jones crying and singing alone in her underwear to demonstrate how lonely you are. Movie clips aren't there to illustrate how you feel or to just sound pretty. They're there for you to talk about, ridicule, dissect, or celebrate. So use them wisely.

Finally, a few words about poetry, books, and other written materials: As with music, a lot of literature is in the public domain, which means you can read it aloud on your show. Most written work under Creative Commons licenses is also podsafe. Anything a copyright holder has given you permission to use is absolutely fine. And in specific instances—such as literary criticism—reading a line or two from a text may fall under fair use. Just be sure in all the above cases to credit the book and author, and when in doubt, consult an attorney.

25

Determine the Best Length for Your Show

On the topic of time, Jolenta and I have been asked more than once why By the Book episodes aren't longer. Some listeners say they enjoy our company so much that they want to spend more than forty minutes with us. But do they really?

A number of studies suggest that most listeners prefer podcasts that are twenty to forty minutes long. That's because the average listener spends twenty to forty minutes on the main activities they do while listening to podcasts: exercising, commuting to work, getting ready in the morning, tidying the house, or making dinner. I have a theory that this time range is also popular because it matches how audiences have been trained to consume TV since birth (a half-hour TV comedy is twenty minutes minus the ads; an hour-long TV drama is forty minutes minus ads).

You may be thinking, *But but but, My Favorite Murder is sometimes nearly an hour and a half long, and so are a bunch of other shows.* You are correct, but when it comes to successful podcasts, these shows tend to be the exception, not the rule. More often than not, longer shows have fat that could stand to be trimmed. They drag rather than have momentum. And that drag can be tough for new listeners to jump into (or old listeners to stay interested in).

Alternatively, you might be thinking, *But but but, Side Hustle School is under six minutes! And A Little Happier is only two minutes! Short shows are great!* Indeed, short shows can be a fun, snappy taste of something delicious. There are many short shows I love. But warning: Shorter shows tend to have a harder time attracting advertisers (because, let's be honest, it's odd for listeners to hear an ad in a show that's the same length as the episode). Of course, if you don't plan to have advertisers in your show, no problem!

All that being said, I've come across dozens of shows that are too long, too rambly, too inclusive of tangents that don't belong there, too similar to a never-ending speech rather than a delicious listen—and absolutely zero that I've considered too short.

My advice: Start out making a show that clocks in around twenty minutes. You can always make it longer later, but shorter is the best way to start out. Why?

1. It's easier to manage when you're trying to manage everything. Let's presume that, like most podcasters, you're doing everything from the writing and hosting to guest-booking and editing. Do you really want to write a fifty-page script? Do you really want to record *and* edit down two hours of audio? No, of course you don't. You're only one person, and that's too much to handle day after day, week after week. You're going to burn yourself out.

2. It will train you to make every minute count. When you put a time restraint on yourself, you'll be less likely to record yourself yammering on and on or going off topic. You'll make a show that's tighter, cleaner, and with better momentum. Years ago, one of the best compliments I'd ever heard of a

short story was "It's beautiful because every word must be." Make sure that your podcast is the same way. Make sure that every word must be.

How Long Are All the Other Podcasts Out There?

Based on a sample of ten million episodes in 2018, Pacific Content found that the median podcast duration was 38 minutes and 42 seconds.

The average length would actually be quite a bit shorter, if not for the following four categories: video games, other games, games and hobbies (yes, I realize that's a lot of different ways of saying "gaming"), and music. Pacific Content's study found that shows in these categories averaged between 60 and 75 minutes per episode.

Shows that were the shortest were in the categories of language lessons, education, training, and children's content, with all four clocking in at under 20 minutes per episode.

26

Know What Listeners Love

After talking through the basics of show production with aspiring podcasters, I sometimes hear this: "Hey! There seems to be a lot of wiggle room in your advice. You keep telling me that I should be myself and focus on a topic that I'm passionate about and use my own voice. But are there things that every podcaster should do that all listeners love?"

Of course, no two listeners are the same. There are listeners who want to listen to the BBC 24/7 and listeners who exclusively listen to reality TV recap podcasts on the days after their favorite shows air.

But I'm going to tell you a secret: Regardless of whether your show follows the adventures of a competitive monster-truck driver or divulges the secret organizing tips of a stay-at-home dad, there are, in fact, some things that listeners almost universally like. Here are a few of them:

- Solid takeaways. Listeners like conclusions and lessons from their content; give it to them!

- Revealing hosts. Lots of hosts relay facts—but the best ones reveal aspects of themselves, from their personal histories and obsessions to their shortcomings and embarrassments. When they do, listeners find them more relatable. They want their hosts to be human, not perfect.

- A mix of predictability and surprises. This is where the afore-mentioned structure comes in handy. Listeners like know-ing what to expect in each episode, but they also like the occasional deviation from the structure. Likewise with a host's personality. They want a host who's consistently them-self but also shows surprising opinions or sides of their per-sonality from time to time.

Now, there's a good chance you're rolling your eyes at this list of universal crowd-pleasers I've put together. In speaking to classrooms and at conferences, I've gotten a lot of the roly-poly eyes.

For example, comedians I've talked to have asked, "Why do I need **solid takeaways**? Aren't I just here to entertain? I'm not NPR!" Trust me, I'm not asking you to be NPR. But if you can help listeners learn something or look at the world differently, they'll feel that much more connected to you and your show. Consider, for example, *The Daily Show*, which is both a satirical TV show and a podcast. Each episode presents current events in a hilarious way—but the show does far more than that: It provides the clear opinions of Trevor Noah and the producers on what is right and wrong in the world.

On the topic of being **revealing**, I've heard professors (and CEOs and engineers) say, "Hey, I'm a respected scholar/CEO/engineer, and I just want to share my knowledge about thirteenth-century rural shoe merchants/quarterly returns/structural supports with the masses! Why do I have to show vulnerability?"

Let me tell you why: Even a scholar is a person. Take, for example, the great Malcolm Gladwell, host of Revisionist History. On the surface, it may seem that each episode of his show is just a look at history from a slightly different angle. But look closer and you'll realize it's more than that: It's a look at the world through Malcolm Gladwell's eyes—as the son of two scholars, as a half-Jamaican Canadian, as a sports fanatic and music lover and admitted control freak (for more on this last point, listen to his episode titled "Are You Lonesome Tonight?"). Revisionist History is a show about a human with his own obsessions and peculiarities.

As for the mix of **predictability and surprises**, just play peek-a-boo with a toddler. The toddler knows you're going to disappear and come back. That's the consistency. But the surprise is where and when you'll come back. Will it be over the top of your hands? Between your hands? Will it be after a three-second pause or a split second? Most of us aren't that different from toddlers. For more on predictability and surprises, look back at chapters 6 and 7 on format (page 33) and structure (page 39).

Of course, there are lots of other things listeners love (this book is filled with them!), but at the bare minimum, focus on these (and avoid with a passion any of the mistakes laid out in the next chapter).

27

Know What Listeners Hate

Friends, I'm a lover, not a hater. And I really don't want to dwell on the horrible parts of life or podcasting. But I also believe that shining a light on what's awful in life can help us to stop doing those awful things—whether it's misogyny or making horrible decisions with your podcast. And yes, there are some podcasting mistakes that listeners universally tend to hate. They include:

* Lousy sound quality. Bad audio means everything from extreme volume changes to background noise to that echo-y sound that says your show was made in a garage by amateurs who don't care.

* Overproduced audio. From music to "realistic" sounds (birds chirping, car engines revving, soup pots bubbling) to reverberating audio effects, there is such a thing as too much of a good thing.

* Inconsistency—in tone, quality, and distribution schedule.

* A lack of empathy for your listeners. Empathy means not just talking to yourself or for yourself, but also talking to them.

Of course, there are other things listeners hate as well: too many obscure references, dead air, too much self-promotion—the list goes on and on. But the four mistakes I see most often that listeners hate are these. Let's walk through them.

Horrible audio quality. I can't restate enough how off-putting it is. Sound is the one single sense that's being engaged when someone listens to a podcast. There aren't pretty visuals to fall back on. There's no sweet old grandma giving you a bear hug or the smell of banana bread baking in the oven to keep you engaged beyond what's in your ears. It's just the listener and the sound, so the sound must be the very best it can be.

I know this step isn't always easy. Sometimes the space you're recording in isn't as quiet as you thought it was. Maybe you accidentally talked into the mic incorrectly or all your guests could only join you by cell phone while driving in traffic. Perhaps you didn't have time to level out your audio. But consider this: How many times have you listened to a podcast with terrible audio quality and immediately called a friend and insisted, "You absolutely must listen to this crappy-sounding podcast"? I'm guessing the answer is never. Don't put your podcast in the same predicament as this imaginary crappy show. You and your listeners deserve better.

Overproduced shows. Special effects can be fun. Who doesn't like it when a show has original music to introduce each segment or the occasional sound effect that says, "We're now accepting phone calls from listeners"? But when overdone, special effects can quickly turn the corner from amusing to distracting to downright irritating. Think about the shock-jock morning-drive shows that try to hold your attention between songs and ads with cowbells, doorbells, laugh tracks, TV-theme-song snippets, and snare drums to punctuate jokes. They're only on for a few minutes at a time, which is why they're palatable. But try to emulate them for an entire forty-minute show and your average listener may begin to feel they're losing their mind.

This isn't to say that all special effects are bad. Shows like Radiolab create entire, immersive worlds from them. But there's a fine line between immersive audio and overproduced landfills of sound. So be deliberate in your use of bells and whistles. Don't use sound effects every twenty seconds. Don't drop in the sound of a record scratch every time someone says something awkward. And definitely don't run music and sound effects under half your show.

Inconsistency. Inconsistency is another hugely common mistake with podcasters, and it's an absolute deal breaker for many listeners. Inconsistency can bleed into many areas, including the structure of the show, the hosting team, and the way a show is distributed.

In the case of structure, you may feel like I'm beating a dead horse by now, but it's no joke. A show needs a consistent shape, not just a mess of talking. Think about it: If listeners wanted a mess of talking, they wouldn't be turning on a podcast. There are plenty of places in the real world they can find that: a coffee shop, a bus, a street corner, literally anywhere that has humans. Be the thing they escape to, not put up with.

With regard to the inconsistency of hosting teams, imagine if you listened to a show for the past four weeks that was hosted by Lisa and June. In those four weeks, you began to really enjoy the rapport between these two women and feel connected to each host. But then imagine if they began swapping out June for Shamya and Lisa for Clarice. Would you still want to go back to the show week after week? I'm guessing your answer is no.

And then there are inconsistency issues around the distribution of a show. Some new podcasters will eagerly release new episodes as soon as they're done tirelessly working on them—regardless of what day of the week it is or when their last episode came out. This can be confusing and frustrating for listeners, who are accustomed to their shows coming out every day, every week, every other week, or on some other consistent schedule. Eventually, they may very well lose interest in keeping up with your haphazard release schedule and just move on to other shows. For more on this topic, refer to the next chapter.

Finally, let's talk about a lack of empathy. A lot of podcasters love the sound of their own voices, and what's not to love? As I've said many times before, your voice is a gift. But if it's not used correctly, it can feel like a nightmare to your potential listeners. Put yourself in their shoes. Are you only talking about yourself to yourself, or are you acknowledging that they're out there, giving their ears to you? Are you situating them in a time and place in every episode, or presuming they'll find their way without you? Are you making something you would listen to if you didn't know yourself? Think about your listeners. Show them you care about them, that you're grateful for them, and that you listen to them, just as they listen to you. Answer their letters on air. Fold their feedback into your ad spots, like Gretchen Rubin does on Happier. Center whole episodes on their unique relationship with your subject matter, like Dan Pashman does on The Sporkful. And in every single episode, thank them for listening. If you don't, they may choose one of the other one million–plus podcasts to listen to instead—those in which the hosts actually show they care.

Part 6

SHARE IT

Create a Release Schedule

Gentle readers, we're getting very close to magic time: the time when you put your beautiful, funny, strange, unique creation out into the world. But before we get to that, we have a few more steps. Let's begin with your release schedule.

Now, there are a lot of schools of thought on this. Some folks will tell you that the more episodes you release each week, the better. Others will say a release schedule doesn't matter, because podcasts are listened to on demand, at listeners' whims. My thought on the matter: Ignore that advice. Instead, think about what you can do well and make sure you're consistent.

Listeners want to know when to expect their podcast, just as they'd want to know when their favorite TV show is on every week or when their favorite sport will begin being broadcast each season. This means not just the day, but also the time of day.

How important is this to listeners?

Consider this: Years ago, *Slate* was a day late putting up an episode of their popular roundtable show Political Gabfest. Not days. Not weeks. One day. It didn't take long for listeners to start reaching out to express confusion, concern, and just flat-out irritation. Among them: a late-night TV show host who said he relied on the podcast to help him plan his own television program. His name was Stephen Colbert, and the show he was referring to was *The Colbert Report*.

Of course, this is an extreme example. Not all podcasts have famous people writing in to complain after the podcast is a day late. But all podcasts with a loyal following should be warned that their listeners will notice if they deviate from their schedules.

My recommendation (this gets back to doing what you can do well): Start production on your show. Once you're done with the pilot (which will take more time than any other episode you make), see how long it takes to make the following three episodes. Does it take two days per episode? Or does it take two weeks? Establish a regular writing/hosting/editing schedule that you can stick to. Finally, when you have your production schedule nailed down, you can determine your release schedule (and, bonus, you'll have a few extra episodes in the can in case you get sick or other life issues get in the way of your schedule).

But a warning: Don't be overly ambitious. Yes, some shows come out several times a week, or even daily, but your show doesn't have to, even if your first four episodes suggest it's possible.

On the flip side: Don't release too infrequently. If your show comes out only once per month or once every other month, old listeners may forget about you and new listeners may have a hard time discovering you. On top of that, there's a chance that the podcast app your listeners use will stop downloading new episodes to their feed if more than a month passes between releases.

The sweet spot: once a week, or once every other week if that's more doable. That will allow you to become a part of your listeners' weekly or biweekly listening habits and hopefully give you the time to make your show well.

Note: The above advice applies to most podcasts, but there are some exceptions to the rules. Example: a suspenseful short-run series, like Empire on Blood, a true-crime podcast released in 2018 about a man falsely accused of double homicide. Those of us working on the show decided that, because of the genre and pacing of the story, listeners would likely want to binge it rather than wait even a day between episodes. And so we released all the episodes at once. Bonus: When you binge-drop a show, you have the chance to lift the download numbers of all your episodes (not just the first) right out of the gate, because people who like your show will just keep hitting the *play* button.

That's not to say that all short-run series should drop all their episodes at once. Weekly releases are still the most common in the podcasting world, regardless of whether they're ongoing shows, seasonal shows, or a short-run series.

And one final note on release schedules: Be clear with your listeners. If your show comes out weekly, let them know that you'll be back next week. If your show is seasonal, tell them when the next season will begin. If your show is a short-run series, thank them for joining you for the duration of the show.

Consistency + communication = your perfect release schedule.

Ongoing, Seasonal, and Short-run Series

Here are the differences among three common types of series:

ONGOING SERIES: This is a show that has no foreseeable end. It comes out once per week, once every other week, several times a week, or daily. These kinds of shows can cover any topic, but are often news shows, talk shows, or interview shows. Examples: Call Your Girlfriend, The Waves.

SEASONAL SHOW: This kind of show is like a TV series. It has a season per year, or maybe even two or three seasons per year. Between seasons, there may be bonus content released, reruns, or nothing at all. Examples: Still Processing, Serial.

SHORT-RUN SERIES: This is a show that's a limited-run series by design. In the world of TV, it would be called a miniseries. Many true-crime documentaries and fiction podcasts are short-run series. Examples: Dirty John, 36 Questions.

29

Make Enticing Show Art

It's time to talk about art! Pretty, poppy, enticing art!

I know, I know. You're an audio artist, not a graphic artist. But trust me, this is important. In order to publish your show, you'll need show art. The show art will appear in feeds. If you're ever written up, it will appear in blog posts and articles. In most cases, it will be the first thing potential listeners will know about your show. And if it doesn't look good, they won't hit the *play* button on your show, much less subscribe to it.

So dedicate some real time to this. Open any podcast app and look at the show tiles of other podcasts out there. What looks enticing to you, and what looks cheap? What show tiles do you barely notice, and which ones do you want to copy?

More than likely, you're finding yourself drawn to show art that isn't overly complicated; to images that are obvious and need no interpretation. The titles of the shows are clear and easy to read. Everything screams, "This is what I am and you should listen to me!" and you're thinking, *Yeah, I will listen to you*.

On the flip side, I'm willing to bet that you're scrolling past any show art that features intricate patterns, flowery fonts, and confusing images. That's because too much visual noise doesn't hold a viewer's attention, and anything that's too hard to interpret isn't worth the time of most people scrolling through Apple Podcasts or Stitcher.

But other than straight-up copy the good art out there (please don't do this), how can you avoid making bad art?

1. Don't make your art for the big screen. Yes, you can and should make it on any size computer screen that works for you. But keep in mind that 99 percent of the time your listeners will be seeing your art not as a giant graphic on a big screen but as a tiny square on a tiny screen. That tiny square will be less than one square inch and appear alongside hundreds of other images that are also less than one square inch. So make the most of your tiny little square, and make it pop.

2. Make sure people can read the words. A very large percentage of podcasts out there have show tiles with words that are hard to decipher. The fonts are curly and delicate, the text color blends in with the background, or there's just too much else in the tiny square that competes with the words. Don't make people wonder if your show is called Only God Can Judge or Only God Can Fudge. If your show is about fudge and religion, make it clear!

3. Don't be afraid of minimalism. A silhouette with words is fine. A crisp photo of you alongside the show title is great. One graphic image of an object and some text does the trick. In some cases, just the name of the show in a strong bold font is perfect. Start with the bare minimum, then add more. Not the other way around.

4. Keep the message consistent. Once you decide on your art, use the same color palette and image (or similar images) across all your branding and social media. That includes Twitter, Facebook, your show's web page, press releases, business cards, and everywhere else your show is in the world.

5. If you're struggling, and can afford one, seek out an expert. There are designers for hire all over the Internet. Some are quite affordable and prolific, churning out dozens of designs a month. Others are pricier and more full-service, creating "brand identity" across everything from your show tile to your promotional merchandise. And quite a few are just students and recent grads looking to build their portfolios. Fortunately, all of them have the potential to bring your show art beautifully to life. But don't go in blindly. Look at everything else they've made and talk to them frankly about their creative process, timeline, and rate.

30

Write Catchy Episode Titles and Descriptions

You can't judge a book by its cover, but you may be more likely to open it if the art is good. The same applies to titles. Would you rather open a book with the title *Horses* or *The Secret Language of Horses?* I'm guessing the latter. Don't you want to know how horses talk? I do!

But the sad fact is that a lot of podcasters treat their episode titles as an afterthought. When it's all in the can, they'll throw a subject on top and call it the title. But remember: A subject is just a subject; it's not a story and it certainly isn't enticing on its own. Be enticing!

Another common mistake is to title an episode first, before it's recorded and edited. But what if something really funny happens during the recording? What if something truly unusual is revealed about a guest? Shouldn't that be in the title? Of course it should!

So, rather than just name an episode after a guest who appears on your show ("DeShawn Smith"), choose a title derived from something

DeShawn Smith says in your interview with him that listeners will be intrigued by ("DeShawn Smith on What Makes Him Cry").

Note: If you want your audience to listen to the episodes of your show in a specific order, be sure to add an episode number to the top of each title (Ep. 1: "Surprise! We're Pregnant!," Ep. 2: "Morning Sickness," Ep. 3: "The First Prenatal Checkup," and so on). This is especially important with stories that are serialized.

Now, let's move on to episode descriptions. As with episode titles, you'll want your episode descriptions to hook people and make clear that there's a story. But on top of that, you'll want to include any relevant words that will come up in a search. That way, your show will be easier for listeners to discover.

For example, if your episode focuses on a notable person, include that person's name and job title ("Leona See, President of the American Velvet Painting Club"). If your episode focuses on a historic event, be sure to include that. Include anything that people will be searching for who are interested in your episode's topic. But don't write a whole essay and don't bury the lede. If it's over ten sentences, it's too long. Make things clear, exciting, and brief.

Finally, be sure that your episode descriptions include all your contact information, links to your social media handles and website, and thanks to any advertisers you have. All of these things will improve your discoverability and make it easier for your listeners to reach you.

31

Distribute Your Podcast

You're at an extraordinary point in the podcasting process: the point when you have everything you need to put your podcast out into the world. You have show art and a release schedule. You have a show title and episode titles. And, of course, you have a bunch of great audio that you've edited together into great stories and great episodes. Now what? How does an episode get off your computer and onto your listeners' devices? Rest assured, it takes only four easy steps!

1. Save Your Episode in the Right Format

Most likely, you recorded and edited your episode in Waveform Audio Format (WAV). But when it comes time to distribute your show, you'll need to export it as an MP3 file. Here's why.

WAV files are an older format and record audio without losing quality. But the files are huge! A minute of audio in WAV format can be 10 MBs to 16 MBs, making a 30-minute episode almost 0.5 GB! While that's small for a desktop computer, that's a huge file for a mobile phone or tablet.

An MP3 file, on the other hand, is a compressed format that throws away unimportant audio information to make a file much smaller. A thirty-minute episode in MP3 format will typically be a tenth of the size of a WAV, making MP3 much better for distribution and mobile devices. This is the format you'll need for hosting and syndication of your show.

2. Choose a Hosting Platform

After you save your finished episode as an MP3, your next step is to create a destination where people can listen to that MP3.

The easiest way is to use a podcast-centric hosting solution that provides bloglike pages, feeds, metadata, and metrics all in one place. Far and away the most popular is Libsyn (which is famous for its ease of use for beginners), but there are many others, like Podbean, Blubrry, and SoundCloud.

An alternative is to create a blog site and use that site to store MP3-encoded audio files. Many online blog services or platforms already have audio/podcast hosting add-ons or options. For example, the popular WordPress open-source blogging platform and their hosted WordPress.com site have simple options to host/set up your podcast. Commercial services like Wix.com or Squarespace also offer simple setup and inclusion of podcast or audio content. The benefits of a blog site are that it gives more options for creativity and the ability to continue your page if you ever stop podcasting. The biggest drawback is that it's more to learn and more to manage.

3. Set Up Your Feed

Once you've created or decided on a place to host the podcast, setting up the feed is the next step. Also called an RSS feed (RSS stands for

Really Simple Syndication), a feed is a list of episodes and where to find them. The feed also carries important additional information (often called metadata), such as title, author, summaries/descriptions, cover artwork, categories, and duration. When you release a new episode, you just add another entry to your feed. Most blogging or hosting platforms, like Libsyn, make adding all this information simple and automatic.

4. Syndicate

Now that you have your feed, you'll want to submit your podcast and its feed to as many places that allow you to find podcasts as possible. This process is called syndication.

Submit your podcast episode feed to Apple Podcasts, Google Podcasts, Stitcher, Spotify, and possibly several others. There are great tutorials online for how to do this, and if you're using a podcast-specific hosting platform (like Libsyn), they all offer automated upload and syndication to popular podcast sources.

You typically need to submit your feed only once. Apple Podcasts, Google Podcasts, or other stores will approve your content after a brief review period. This ensures that your podcast really is what you've said it is. Then, once accepted, the magic of RSS allows you to upload a new episode and have it appear in every store you have registered with!

The Network Option

Now, releasing a show via Libsyn, SoundCloud, or any other hosting platform targeting indie podcasters is a fine way to go. But for some podcasters, it's just a stepping-stone. They want to join a network.

After all, networks have sales teams, production teams, accountants, lawyers, marketing specialists, studios, equipment, and large platforms that almost always guarantee listenership in the tens of thousands (if not hundreds of thousands).

But while there are many podcasting networks in the U.S. (from stand-alone companies to publishers and radio stations), joining a network isn't easy. Most networks won't consider pitches from people who don't have a proven track record in podcasting, a preexisting audience, or fame. And most are unwilling to bring on indie shows that have fewer than fifty thousand downloads per episode. So how do you join a network if you don't have a huge audience?

I was able to get my foot in the door by being a full-time employee at two large networks—first WNYC and then Panoply. At each network, I was given the opportunity to pitch show ideas, and fortunate that my ideas were green-lit. In a lot of ways, I was living the dream.

But there's a trade-off to entering the network game the way I did, and that's that you most likely won't be allowed to own your feed, your episodes, the name of your show, your show's social media feeds, spin-off projects, or anything else related to the intellectual property of your show. Your network will consider your show their property, and they'll consider you a staff member who works on it—even if the idea was something you dreamed about long before the network existed. In turn, if you leave the network, you won't be able to keep the name of the show or back episodes or show art. And you absolutely won't be able to profit from any books, movies, or TV shows that pay for the adaptation rights—that money will go to your network.

Some podcasters have been able to work around this. In rare cases, as in Another Round, the hosts were able to get the rights back from the network (BuzzFeed) at no cost. In other cases, podcasters have been able to buy their rights back and take the show elsewhere or make it on their own. And of course, there have been hosts who've abandoned their shows, gone on to make a similar show with a different name, and launched in a whole new feed with a whole new network (such as Reply All, from the makers of TLDR, and Fiasco, from the makers of Slow Burn).

In the case of By the Book, when Panoply chose to close their content arm at the end of 2018, they sold the show to Stitcher (at which point, Jolenta and I, with the help of our fantastic agent Liz Parker, were able to negotiate terms that allowed us to retain the rights to certain By the Book adaptations).

None of this is to say that networks aren't worth working with. I love working with networks! I wouldn't be where I am today without them. But go in knowing up front what you'll be able to keep, what you'll lose, and how they'll help you.

Now, you might have noticed that I haven't mentioned a word about money in this chapter—despite the fact that distribution and money are often closely intertwined. Not to worry. I know money is something that a lot of podcasters are curious about, and that's why I set aside a whole chapter for the topic. Read on for that.

What About International Distribution?

I'm often asked about the state of podcasting outside the United States. Are there networks? Is there a way to make a podcast in the U.K. or New Zealand or Norway? The good news: You can absolutely make a podcast anywhere in the world! There are outstanding podcasts in the U.K. (shout-out to A Gay & a NonGay, hosted by my former co-host James Barr and his friend Dan Hudson) and Australia (I'd be remiss not to mention the international phenomenon The Teacher's Pet), and pretty much everywhere else that computers, editing software, and the Internet exist.

But while the United States has dozens of networks that make and distribute podcasts, the story is different internationally. In the

U.K., for example, there's really only one major audio network: the BBC. And in other countries, the most successful podcasts tend to be linked to just a few outlets and publications (e.g., The Teacher's Pet was a production of the newspaper *The Australian*).

That's mainly because the listenership is lower. According to the 2019 Infinite Dial Study by Edison Research, 32 percent of Americans listen to podcasts monthly. But head across the pond to the U.K., and you'll find only 5.9 million listeners over the age of 15 (out of an overall population of 66 million), according to research cited by Ofcom.

In other words, it's still very much an indie game internationally. But indie isn't necessarily bad. For example, the indie U.K. podcast My Dad Wrote a Porno boasts more than 150 million downloads, and other indie U.K. podcasts like The Guilty Feminist have garnered international acclaim.

Even more encouraging: New international podcasting awards and conferences are popping up every year, while major international outlets like The Guardian *have begun featuring podcasts on best-of lists every week. Why not get in while the pool is relatively small and visibility is growing? Your podcast could be the next headline maker.*

Think About Monetization

Friends, I don't want to be a Negative Nancy, but I do have to tell you something firmly and clearly: The vast majority of podcasts don't make money. This may come as a surprise, considering all the headlines about the podcasting boom. And don't get me wrong, there are indeed podcasting dollars out there. In fact, PricewaterhouseCoopers (PwC) and the Interactive Advertising Bureau (IAB) predict that U.S. ad spending for podcasts will double from an estimated $314 million in 2017 to $659 million in 2020. But the sad fact is that it's still hard for an indie podcaster to get their hands on that money.

Here's why:

1. Most advertisers are still gun-shy about podcasts. Podcasting is a new medium to them, especially compared to print ads, TV spots, and radio commercials.
2. The advertisers who are comfortable with podcasts generally prefer to work with shows with large audiences, sales departments, and accountants, which means that most are working with networks.

This isn't to say that monetization is impossible for an indie podcaster. I've known several indie podcasters who've managed to make money. A few of them—like Megan Tan of Millennial—have even told me they were able to live off their podcast profits (though in Megan's case, managing the books became another giant job on top of making and marketing her show, which is why she eventually joined Radiotopia).

If you're determined to make money, there are a few routes you can take:

1. Listener support. In each episode of your show, ask your listeners to donate to you via a site like Patreon or Kickstarter. In exchange for donations, podcasters usually give their listeners gifts, shout-outs on the show, or other rewards.

2. Membership/subscription. Some shows are available to paying members only. In other cases, shows are available to anyone who wants to listen, but members receive ad-free listening, bonus content, early access to episodes, or other options that make it worth a few dollars a month.

3. Advertisers. You know those ads you always hear for Third-Love bras and Casper mattresses on shows? Most of them appear in podcasts within big networks. But there are other advertisers who are willing to appear in smaller shows whose target demographics perfectly match your audience. For example, if you have a show about pregnancy, there are diaper companies, baby food companies, or play spaces that may be interested in advertising on your show.

4. Sponsored content. In sponsored content an advertiser pays for a certain number of episodes or a whole season, usually

in exchange for being central to the storyline of the show. That means that if, say, you have a podcast about cocktails, you could ask Svedka to sponsor a four-part series on vodka cocktails, and later ask Baileys Irish Cream to sponsor a St. Patrick's Day cocktail series, and so on. But note: When going this route, you must be willing to let the brand make editorial decisions about your content, which may slow down your production process and dampen your vision for your show.

In the first two cases, you need to have listeners who truly feel invested in you and in your show. If you're lucky, you may end up like Opening Arguments, a podcast that explains the law behind the news and earned $1,721 per month in 2016 from its loyal donors. And if you're really really really lucky, you may end up like Last Podcast on the Left, the true-crime series that earned roughly $25K per month from its 4,300 Patreon supporters as of 2017.

As for the latter two models, my suggestion is to first build an audience of five thousand dedicated listeners per episode (your hosting platform will be able to tell you about your numbers of unique listeners, subscribers, and so on) and then learn as much as you can about those listeners (such as their gender, age, race, and geography). Then, take that information to potential advertisers, prepare to hear a lot of people say no, and when you finally hear yes, get your rates in writing and keep meticulous books.

Finally, if none of the above options feel like a fit for you, don't lose hope. Keep up-to-date on what various distribution platforms are offering. More and more, like Anchor and Megaphone, are experimenting with how to place ads in shows with smaller audiences. And as the podcasting world gets more established, more advertisers will seek out podcasters who make great content and have strong listener bases—some, in fact, already are!

How Much Advertisers Pay for Spots on Podcasts

Podcast advertisements are usually calculated on a CPM basis. CPM stands for "cost per mil" (*mil* is derived from the Latin word meaning "thousand"—so another way to say this would be "cost per thousand"). It works like this: You and the advertiser determine how much money they are willing to pay for each thousand downloads a new episode of your show receives, usually over the course of a month. So, if each episode of your show receives 10,000 downloads in its first month and your CPM is $20, that means you'd earn $200 for that one ad appearing in one new episode of your show. CPM rates usually range from $15 to $50, with the higher rates going to shows with the most downloads.

Part 7

GROW IT

33

Prioritize Promotion

I was recently at one of the nation's most respected audio festivals, sitting in the audience while a panel onstage discussed the ups and downs of indie podcasting. The moderator guided the three independent podcasters through several topics—asking what each show was about, whether any of them had outside production help, how they managed their time, and so on. Eventually she got to the topic of promotion. "How do you spread the word about your show?" she asked.

The first panelist responded firmly, saying, "I'm an artist. My job is to be a creator, not to be a marketing firm."

The other two panelists nodded along. The second said, "I have a full-time job, and I make this show; I barely have time to do anything after that."

The third panelist said, "I like to think that if I make a good product that I love, people will just come to it." She pointed to the fact that she had more than five hundred listeners as proof of her theory.

Now, I don't mean to poo-poo any of these indie podcasters. I have so much admiration for the hard work they put into making their shows with little to no help. It takes incredible determination.

But here's the thing: I think they're wrong. If you want listeners (and I'm guessing the vast majority of you reading this do), then it's absolutely necessary that you promote your podcast.

That's because the means of discoverability are very limited in the world of podcasting. People don't just turn on the radio or TV and stumble across you. Unless you're with a major network with a well-funded marketing department, they won't hear ads for your show or see billboards with your face on them. Your show will not just magically appear on their phones or play in their earbuds. The onus is on you to get the word out—every week, for several hours a week.

I know it sounds exhausting. I get it. I used to feel the same way. Like panelist number two, I used to point to my sixty-plus-hour workweek and say, "How could anyone also ask me to promote my show on top of everything else I do?"

I also understand that self-promotion can feel embarrassing. What polite person on the planet wants to go out into the world yelling, "Listen to me! I have so many interesting things to say that I actually make recordings of myself saying them, and I think you should listen to those recordings in your precious spare time!"

But listen. It's important. And even with limited time, it's doable. You can fold promotional work into the rest of your show production work. You can do it along with the other things you already do every day for fun (I'll tell you more about how in the coming chapters). And if you change your perspective on things, you might even come to enjoy it. Much to my own shock, I have. I sincerely believe you can reach this point too.

Don't believe me? Let's look back at that third panelist. She said she had more than five hundred listeners. That's way more friends than most of us have, which means she really was getting people beyond her inner circle to listen to her show. But imagine how many more she'd have if she stopped saying, "If I make a good product that I love, people will just come to it," and instead said, "I love my show so much, and pour so much of myself into it, that I want to introduce it to more people who will love it as well."

Other scripts that might work for you:

- "I know my show can help people, and I want to get it to the people it can help."
- "I wish I'd had a show like this to listen to when I first embarked on my profession."
- "I have a feeling my show will make a lot of people feel less alone."
- "There are a lot of women I know who love this topic, but it seems there are almost exclusively men talking about it. I want those women to know there are people acknowledging their perspective."

Of course, these are just a few examples. There are hundreds more. But I don't need to list them all for you. If you look back to the beginning of this book, you'll see that you already know what to say. Remember when I asked you why you wanted to make a show, and who it was for? That's your script, and those are your people. Share your show, use your own words. I assure you that, eventually, Louise and Anwar and whoever else is sitting in your audience will be grateful you told them about it.

34

Build Community

For a lot of podcasters, it doesn't matter how many ways I ask them to change their mind-set around promotion. They still feel weird about it. But then I say the word "community," and something clicks.

"Community" sounds welcoming. "Community" says, "We're in this together." "Community" doesn't feel like "Hey, listen to me toot my own horn." It sounds like "Friends, let's build this thing together." And that's because community is more than listeners. It's people who count on each other and feel they're part of something bigger— something they want to spread the word about and share with the people who trust them (an achievement no billboard has ever claimed to do).

With all the shows I've co-hosted and produced, I've come to love my community members with an ardor that borders on nutty. I've gotten to know them by name and location, and many of them have followed me from one show to the next (I'm talking to you, Ken Ronkowitz in New Jersey). And these listeners have done far more than just subscribe and download (which are already huge gifts); they've created content for my shows in the form of the stories they've shared.

They've helped me to be a better host through their compliments and criticisms. They've taught me and other listeners to see the world differently. And they've promoted their favorite episodes on social media and even written blog posts and articles encouraging other people to listen to my work.

But how do you build your dream community? How do you go from speaking into a microphone to having people feel a connection with you and each other and your show? How do you get a person who stumbled across your podcast by chance to come back again and again and tell all their friends to subscribe? There's no magic formula, but there are a few things I've found that work. I'm going to break them down into three distinct categories: what to do in your podcast, what to do outside your podcast, and what your listeners can do for you. Here goes.

Build Engagement Within Your Podcast

* Give your listeners ways to reach out to you. Set up a phone number and email address just for your show. Both are easy to do with Google. Make sure the phone number is always set to go to voicemail and has a friendly greeting—you don't want to actually have to talk to everyone who calls! In each episode of your show, mention the contact methods, along with a prompt of why they should call or write. Also include these contact methods in your show notes.

* Ask your listeners to tell you about their experiences with what you're covering on your show. For example, on *Vanity Fair*'s In the Limelight podcast—which is all about celebrity news and royal gossip—Josh Duboff and Julie Miller ask their listeners to share stories of their own celebrity sightings. The voicemails and letters are sometimes dishy, some-

times reverent, and always full of unexpected details (from the fake name Prince George used to introduce himself to a stranger in a dog park to what Angelina Jolie and her kids wore when they were spotted rock climbing).

* Give your listeners assignments. On Movie Date, Rafer and I ended each episode by playing a movie clip and asking listeners to identify the clip. Each week, listeners from around the world would call and write in with their answers. The only prize for knowing the right answer was having your name read out loud in the next episode if we drew you from the hat. And yet, people called back week after week. Note: You don't have to have the same assignment in every episode of your show. For example, when I was producing Happier with Gretchen Rubin, we once asked listeners to submit haikus about their lives via Twitter. After receiving hundreds, Gretchen and her sister Liz read some out loud on the show, including the listeners' names and Twitter handles, to the great joy of the listeners. And bonus: The hosts' following increased significantly.

* Let listeners reach out to you for advice. Even if you don't consider your show an advice show, think about how you might offer advice through your unique lens. For example, as I mentioned earlier, on Movie Date we had a segment called Movie Therapy. Listeners would call and write in with their life issues, and we would offer up a list of movies or TV shows to help them through what ailed them—whether it was a list of films featuring happy, independent women after a painful breakup, feel-good movies showcasing professional success during a career change, or just a single long-running TV series for new parents suffering through sleepless nights.

- Ask your listeners to give you advice. In every episode of By the Book, Jolenta and I ask listeners to tell us what books they think we should live by next. And every single day, we receive dozens of nominations. That's because people love to help, and they also love to be experts. And above all, they love it when we honor their advice by living by one of their nominated books. Each week, someone writes in saying, "At last! You lived by the book I suggested"—regardless of whether they were the only one to nominate the book, or one of thousands to do so.

- Above all, ask your listeners specific questions in every episode of your show that lead to stories, not opinions or yes/no answers. Opinions are fine, but they're everywhere. Meanwhile, stories are unique to each person yet relatable to the masses. So ask your listeners to tell you about the first time they fell in love, the biggest fish they ever caught, an experience at summer camp, a time when they were most worried about money, and their favorite memory with their favorite grandparent. Ask them about anything that's tangentially related to your show that will lead to genuine engagement with them, and that will make other listeners laugh or nod along and say, "I've been there too."

Build Engagement Outside Your Podcast

- Make a space where your listeners can talk to each other. At By the Book, we have a robust Facebook community of more than ten thousand listeners. We began the community a few weeks after launching our show in the hope that listeners would talk with each other about their own experiences with the books we lived by on the show. But the page has turned into something so much bigger—something that never fails to blow us away. Every day, people log on to seek advice about predicaments in their lives. They give advice and offer support. They share their most painful insecurities and greatest joys and commiserate and congratulate each other. They share photos of themselves and their pets and what their homes and neighborhoods look like. And they've even formed their own book clubs around the world—some of which read self-help books and some that read a wider range of literature.

* Provide listeners with additional content. Create a Twitter handle for your show, as well as a Facebook page and Instagram page. Put out something every day on at least one of these platforms—and ideally, put out several things a day on all of them. Let your listeners see what you're reading, what you're thinking about, and glimpses of your personal life. Show them your recording studio, promote upcoming guests and topics, and let them know when a new episode is coming out. And don't just post; respond back to people who post to you, even if it's just hitting the *like* button on their photos.

* Put on live shows, have meet-ups, create opportunities for listeners to meet you in person. Do these things not with the goal of attracting new listeners, but as a way to build stronger relationships with your existing listeners. Let them see how you move your arms when you talk and the way your nose crinkles when you laugh. Take selfies, give compliments,

provide some entertainment, and more than anything—thank each listener for coming out and for making your show what it is.

Let Your Community Help You Bring Others into the Fold

* In every episode of your show, encourage your listeners to rate and review your podcast in Apple Podcasts, Stitcher, and wherever else they listen. Doing so will help others to find the show, as many podcast platforms are set up with discoverability algorithms based on how frequently listeners interact with your show. And then, from time to time, read some of those reviews out loud and thank your listeners.

* Ask them to tell their friends, family, and co-workers about your show. And don't just ask them in your show. Make sure that every time you write back to your listeners, you end your notes saying: "Thank you so much for listening to the show, and for spreading the word about us to all your friends and family. We so appreciate it!"

If all goes well, your listeners will begin to form their own vocabularies around your show, talk to each other as if they're friends, and talk to you as if they've known you for years. They will look forward to each episode and get others to do the same. You'll have created a space that your listeners needed, and that you needed, even if you didn't know it. You won't just have listeners; you'll have a community.

How Not to Be Heartbroken When Listeners Say Mean Things to You

Friends, I'm trusting that, like me, you'll be lucky enough to have an outstanding community around your show that is excited about you and each other and what you make. But even the best community builder can end up with a handful of listeners who say mean things. For example, in just the past week I've been told that I have a "superiority complex." One listener diagnosed me as a troubled person with deep issues that I'm in denial about. Another said I'm a "bad friend." These insults all came about because I didn't like a book that these specific listeners were fond of. Obviously, it sucks to be called names and accused of things that aren't true. But I have a few coping mechanisms that help:

1.   I try to separate the constructive criticism from the insults. There's a difference between name-calling and feedback that can actually help me be a better podcaster. Someone suggesting that I use more descriptive language or include more dates and names is giving feedback. Someone putting down my character or calling me names is just acting like a jerk.

2.   I remember that listener responses are a gift. Decades ago, I wrote a feature in my college paper that attracted more hate mail than anything the paper had ever published (for the record: The story was called "So Hip It Hurts: When Being Cool Goes Too Far" and it was about the problematic economics of coolness). Hundreds of letters came in, calling me names and saying that my story was clearly written by a loser. I was devastated. But my mother reminded me that I was lucky. "Look at how many people are talking about you! Do you know how many people would kill for that kind of publicity?" Indeed, she was right. What I wrote struck a chord, enough of a chord that people were talking about me. I often reflect on this moment when I'm getting a lot of angry mail.

3.   I don't face my criticism alone. I've always been fortunate to have outstanding co-hosts who commiserate with me when things

get rough. And not only do they commiserate with me, they talk me down from the ledge and sometimes defend me on the show. For example, in the early days of hosting Movie Date, a number of listeners said I laughed too much on the show. They said I sounded unprofessional, like a giggly schoolgirl who couldn't be taken seriously. Eventually, my co-host, Rafer, got so irritated with the criticism that he addressed it on air. He said that he'd read all the letters and heard all the voicemails, and that he had a taped response he wanted to share. Then he played the tape, which was just a long mash-up of me during my jolliest Movie Date moments, laughing and laughing. When the tape stopped, he concluded by saying, "Kristen's laughter is the best thing about this show, and if you're not listening for her laughter, I don't know why you're listening at all."

4. I remember that most of my listeners have good things to say. Well over 90 percent of the mail I've received over the years has been positive. Some of it has been so positive I've cried. But that 5 to 7 percent of critical mail can hurt. Any time I'm getting too down about it, I remember: The percentage of angry letters doesn't actually equal the percentage of angry listeners. I learned this back when I was a teenager, training to be a customer service rep at a call center (a job I genuinely loved). One thing the trainers made clear: The vast majority of satisfied customers will never tell you they're happy with you. But a very large percentage of dissatisfied people will make their irritation known. That means that for every one person who compliments you, there are probably dozens more not saying anything. The dissatisfied people are just louder.

5. I address the listeners on air and in our communities. One other thing I learned at the customer service gig: When you acknowledge someone who's mad at you, try to fix what's wrong, or just listen, they'll usually become more loyal than the customer who was never upset with you in the first place. So write back to them. Let them know you hear them. And from time to time, read their letters on air (with or without Rafer's laugh track mash-up). This won't just make that one listener more satisfied, it will help all your listeners to see you as a human being, and not just a talking head they can throw their anger at.

35

Get the Word Out

At this point you've hopefully achieved a positive mind-set about promoting your show and are feeling totally amped about building your community. Trust me, I'm amped for you! You're gonna do this!

But what else should you do? Will good community members and a good mind-set be enough to promote your show? Alas, the answer is no. You also have to be brave and get the word out. Fortunately for you, you've already proven yourself to be brave. It took bravery to embark on this journey in the first place. And you're going to use that bravery as you take the following seven steps:

1. Tell everyone you know about your show. Do it with snappiness and enthusiasm, using the elevator pitch we discussed earlier in the book. Tell them on Facebook and Twitter and Instagram, always including links to your show. Tell them in person, giving them a business card with links to your show. And make clear what they'll get out of listening, pointing to specific episodes that match their interests.

2. Create a web page. You can do it in an afternoon with a user-friendly site that has its own templates (like Squarespace) or hire someone else to do it if you have some extra cash. A web page does three things for you: It gives people a place to go when you tell them about your show—whether those people are members of the press who want to add you to their latest top ten list, or potential new listeners. It provides a place where rookie podcast listeners can listen to each of your episodes without having to use scary apps (for the two-thirds of Americans not currently listening to podcasts, this is important!). And finally, it increases traffic volume. If you fold popular search terms related to your show's topic into your site (one of the easiest ways to do this is by including a feed of your social media posts), your web page will generate random traffic.

3. Practice guerrilla marketing. When there are conversations happening on Reddit or Facebook or Twitter or anywhere else online about the subject of your show or about podcasting more broadly, jump in and mention your show. Or, start your own conversation by saying something provocative. For example, a couple years back, I decided to go on a Twitter rant about yet another top ten list of great podcasts that only featured shows hosted by men. I asked people online to chime in with their favorite shows hosted by women. The post received thousands of comments in less than a week, and I gained hundreds of new followers.

4. Arrange for promo swaps. A large percentage of podcast listeners say they find out about new shows from the hosts of shows they already listen to. Sometimes hosts just genuinely love another show and will talk about it. Other times the endorsement comes because two hosts have arranged

for a promo swap. In a promo swap, each host will either verbally endorse the other's podcast or play a thirty-second trailer for the other show at the top or bottom of their own show. But how do you arrange a promo swap? You reach out to shows with audiences that have a high likelihood of liking your content. That means if you have a true-crime show, you might want to arrange for promo swaps with other true-crime shows or other shows that target female audiences. Just be mindful of audience size. In most cases, a show with a million listeners won't be interested in swapping promos with a show that has an audience of three hundred, while a show with 750 listeners may be open to the idea.

5. Interview people on your show—people you're genuinely interested in and who also have their own following. That means other show hosts, high-profile experts, influencers, authors, and celebrities. After they're on your show, send them an email that includes a link to the episode, thank them profusely, and ask them to spread the word. If you're feeling especially bold, you can even give them a sample tweet with your episode link to share online. Also, promote the episode on social media, tagging the guest and including an intriguing quote from the interview. More than likely, they'll retweet you or reshare your post in some other way.

6. Pitch yourself as a guest to other shows. Compile a list of shows that have audiences that may also like your show. Aim for shows that are the same size as yours, or just a little bit bigger (as opposed to blockbuster shows with millions of listeners, which rarely bring on up-and-coming podcasters). Reach out by email, and in your pitch, make clear the value you would give to their audience. When you're being

interviewed, be sure to mention your podcast. And after you're on the show, promote your appearance on all your social media channels, tagging the host and hashtagging any commonly searched-for topics. Also promote the interview on your own show. Not only will your efforts drive more people to your interview, and more listeners to your show as a result, they'll also give you examples of interviews you can point to when you pitch yourself to other shows.

7. Turn all your thank-yous into self-promotion. As a show host, you should broadcast your appreciation to the world. In other words, don't just say thank you, write your thank-yous on social media, where they'll be seen and shared and retweeted. I've already mentioned thanking shows that have you on and thanking guests that are on your show. But you should also thank any advertisers you have, tagging them and your show. Thank book authors who've inspired you over the past week the same way. Thank fans who write you. Thank anyone—from small bloggers to large newspapers—that write you up, tagging all the other shows they mention in their piece ("Thank you, XXX, for writing up @ByTheBookPod as one of your favorite shows! How great to be in the company of greats like @RoyalWeddingPod!"). The more you tag, the more likely you'll be retweeted or shared.

How to Pitch Yourself as a Guest on Other Shows

It may feel scary and brazen to reach out to people you don't know and pitch yourself, but trust me, you'll be doing them a favor. That's because podcasters are generally keeping their eye out for new stories. Give them what they want, in the form of you! If they say no, that's their loss.

- In the subject line, write "Guest Pitch" and then just a bit more. ("Podcast Guest Pitch: Food Expert on Tricks for Picky Eaters")

- In the body of the email, introduce yourself and your show. ("Dear Ms. Watson, My name is Dena Ali and I'm the host of a podcast called Happy to Eat You. In each episode of Happy to Eat You, I talk about what I'm excited to eat, and try to get others excited as well.")

- Tell the host that you like their show, and prove it. ("I'm a huge fan of Parenting: The Final Frontier and especially love your episodes involving food, like the one you did on eating in the car with your baby.")

- Pitch your idea and make sure it sounds relevant to their audience. ("I'd love to be a guest on your show, to discuss another food topic: picky little eaters—and strategies for getting them to eat more broadly and with fewer meltdowns.")

- Give at least three examples of what you'll give to their audience. ("Specifically, I'll be able to discuss: the benefits of grocery shopping together, how preparing meals as a family can make food less intimidating, and tricks to disguise scary foods.")

- Include your contact information. ("Please let me know if this would be of interest to you. You may email or phone me at 555-123-4567.")

- Make clear that you'll return the favor. ("I would, of course, enthusiastically promote the episode across all my social media channels and on my own show.")

- In your signature, include a bit more about your show and its prior guests, as well as links to your website and social media feeds.

- Be polite! If you're not saying "please" and "thank you" and saying something nice about them, you're doing it wrong.

- Keep it brief! Get to the point. If it's more than a dozen sentences, it's too long.

- Here's how your completed letter should look:

- Subject line: Podcast Guest Pitch: Food Expert on Tricks for Picky Eaters

Dear Ms. Watson,

My name is Dena Ali and I'm the host of a podcast called Happy to Eat You. In each episode of Happy to Eat You, I talk about what I'm excited to eat, and try to get others excited, as well.

I'm a huge fan of Parenting: The Final Frontier and especially love your episodes involving food, like the one you did on eating in the car with your baby.

I'd love to be a guest on your show, to discuss another food topic: picky little eaters—and strategies for getting them to eat more broadly and with fewer meltdowns. Specifically, I'll be able to discuss:

-the benefits of grocery shopping together
-how preparing meals as a family can make food less
  intimidating
-and tricks to disguise scary foods.

Please let me know if this would be of interest to you. You may email or phone me at 555-123-4567. I would, of course, enthusiastically promote the episode across all my social media channels and on my own show.

Thank you for your time and consideration.

Sincerely,
Dena Ali
Host, Happy to Eat You
Phone: 555-123-4567
Twitter / Instagram / Facebook
www.showwebsiteexample.com

Happy to Eat You is a podcast about loving food enthusiastically, minus any snobbery. Our guests have included Melinda Styles, Duane Jefferson, and Lila Park. In the past year, Happy to Eat You has been downloaded more than 10,000 times.

36

Give Great Interviews

In the last chapter, I suggested pitching yourself to other shows as a guest. But let's say one of those shows actually says yes. Are you prepared to give a great interview?

I'm going to confess something to you here and now: When I first started giving interviews I was absolutely terrible. And no, this is not me being modest. Cross my heart, I was downright lousy.

The first interview I ever gave in front of an audience had nothing to do with podcasting. A local TV station in Minneapolis wanted to talk to a wide range of local voters and future voters about the gubernatorial race. At the time I was only fourteen years old and volunteering with a candidate named Paul Wellstone (hats off to anyone who's familiar with the late Paul Wellstone and the ideals he championed). Apparently, my youthful civic enthusiasm appealed to them.

I don't even remember how I got the gig. All I know is that I spent the majority of my segment staring blankly at the camera as the interviewer asked me question after question that I had no idea how to answer. I was mortified. Meanwhile, the other person brought on to be a commentator (a smart, middle-aged activist who we'll call

Francine) was relaxed and poised as she filled in all the dead air that I created.

At the time, I found Francine baffling. I couldn't help but notice that, regardless of what she was asked, she just talked about the issue she was championing. *Hold on, didn't the interviewer just ask you about term limits? How did you manage to answer the question with your thoughts on immigration?* It was like magic, and I had no idea how she did it.

The next time I was interviewed on air was years later. I was a full-grown adult, working as a public radio producer and still in the early days of co-hosting the Movie Date podcast with Rafer Guzman. The daily news show The Takeaway (which Movie Date was a spin-off of) asked if I would join Rafer in his weekly movie review segments on air. Note: The show was live and national and had two million listeners.

The segment producer told me it would be easy: "The host will just ask you the same questions I've written down, and you'll answer them! Rafer's been doing it for months. You'll just join him and do what he does, but put your own spin on it."

Another producer gave this advice: "Just memorize every question the segment producer prepped you with, and every answer you gave her."

It sounded easy. Answer questions, memorize a few lines. But when I sat down in front of that mic the next morning and the little light came on that said we were live and the host started asking me questions that I hadn't even considered (*Why are you asking about the star's political views, anyway?*), I sounded stiff, incoherent, and confused.

Fortunately for me, The Takeaway wanted to give me another chance. Before it came around, I asked another regular commentator on the show, Beth Kobliner, for advice. Beth is a personal finance wiz and a fantastic interview subject. Her advice more or less matched what I should have taken away from Francine during my teenage interview disaster: *Say what you want, not what you're asked.* More specifically: Know the primary points you think will be important to the listener and steer the conversation to those points by pivoting off the questions rather than answering them directly.

That means that if the interviewer asks about a star's politics ("Isn't Valerie Cane involved in some pretty radical politics lately?") and you actually want to talk about how great it is that she's a black lead in an Oscar-worthy movie, take it there instead. Say, "I think the more important issue here is how the politics of Hollywood casting are changing. For generations, Hollywood has almost exclusively told stories through a white lens. Audiences want diversity and they're finally starting to receive it."

See what I did there? I used the word "politics" as a pivot into a totally different subject: the subject I wanted to talk about and that I thought was more useful to the listeners.

Now, in your case, one thing you should always be pivoting back to in your interviews is your own show—what the show is about, the general feeling people might get if they listen, and some details on specific episodes. Of course, you have to do all this in a way that still sounds like engaging content versus an irritating infomercial.

If all this sounds difficult and scary, rest assured, it gets easier the more you do it. And if you do it well, people will enjoy it!

For example, let's say your show is about crocheting. We'll call your imaginary show Crocheting for Macho Men. Imagine that you pitched yourself as a guest to a small local news show to discuss National Handicrafts Month. On air, the host poses questions to you about scarves, then hats, then blankets. It's just one crocheting project after another and nothing about macho men or your show! The solution: Use one of the topics—let's say blankets—as a pivot.

"It's funny you should bring up blankets, because in my opinion, a blanket is the best project for a macho man to try when he's first embarking on crocheting. The macho men I have on my show regularly tell me that they feel less intimidated by large-scale projects because mistakes are harder to see. A potholder shows everything!"

Then, feel free to reminisce about a particular episode.

Wasn't that fun? Of course it was! It was fun for you because you got to talk about what you wanted to talk about. And it was fun for the listeners because you brought something to that local news show that they wouldn't get from any other guest: a perspective that's uniquely yours. When done well, your interviews will give everyone—including yourself—a gift.

Practice with a Friend!

If you're feeling unsure about your ability to give a good interview, take a cue from all the career advisers out there: Practice being interviewed by a friend. Ask your friend to present you with standard interview questions, some questions out of left field, questions that only tangentially match your expertise, questions that you don't know the answers to, and so on. As you answer the questions, be sure to weave in stories and examples. Be engaging and be an advocate for your show. And continually go back to the main points you know you want to hit. Record the whole thing so you can listen back to what worked, what didn't, and how you could do things differently. Then, do the same exercise again with another friend. The more you practice, the easier it will get.

37

Embrace Your Identity as a Podcaster

In one of my earliest writing classes, I remember being told by my instructor to have business cards made. The recommendation: The cards should just have my name, my email address, and the word "writer."

But I'm not a writer, I remember thinking. Other than writing for my college paper and school literary journals, I was unpublished. No one on the planet would have considered me a writer. Wasn't a business card claiming that title just lying?

But my instructor insisted: "If you don't consider yourself a writer, no one else will. Adopt the title. It's who you are and how you want others to see you."

I'm going to give all of you the same advice: Adopt the title "podcaster." Say it out loud, internalize it. Get your business cards made, with your show title and your job title ("host, executive producer").

But that's just the start. You also have to go to the places that other podcasters go, talk to other podcasters about your work, and present yourself to the world as someone who takes podcasting seriously. Here are some ways to do this:

- Subscribe to newsletters that podcasters subscribe to. That includes *Bello Collective*, *Hot Pod News*, and *Podnews*, to name a few. Podcasting newsletters will keep you in the loop on industry news, familiarize you with the big players in the game, introduce you to new shows, and alert you to jobs, classes, and conferences targeting podcasters. In short, they'll make it easier to talk the talk as well as walk the walk.

- Join Facebook communities. There are dozens of Facebook communities for podcasters and podcast fans. Within these communities, the members discuss everything from equipment, show art, and interview techniques to their favorite shows and hosts. Some communities are specifically for women, people of color, or beginners. Some call themselves support groups. Join a handful of these communities. Look at what's being discussed and the tone of each group. If you don't like a group, leave it. But if you do like it, be an active member. Introduce yourself and your show and ask questions. Weigh in on topics. Help others and let yourself be helped. Eventually, if you're feeling brave, organize a meet-up at a coffee shop or bar for community members in your area.

- Attend conferences. Audio conferences take place every month in cities all across the United States, and new ones pop up every year. As with podcasting Facebook communities, conferences vary wildly, focusing on different aspects of podcasting or different identities of podcasters. Do some research to find out which conferences have missions that fit your needs and panels that speak to your concerns. For example, if you're struggling with sound design, you may want to attend conferences that focus on craft. If you want help growing your audience, look for conferences that have lots of panels on marketing and promotion. Also, pay attention to who will be presenting at each conference. Are they people whose work you admire and want to learn from? Or are they people you've never heard of?

- Reach out to people you admire. Conferences are a great place to meet podcasters you admire in person, but there are other ways to meet these people as well. Take a cue from all the young people who reach out to me: Just send an email. Every month, several write asking if they can take me out for a cup of coffee, talk to me about my work, and in the best cases, offer to be of service in some way (by committing to helping the voices of women and people of color be heard on their campus, offering to help me spread the word about one of my shows, and so on). Some of them know me from the shows I host. Others have heard me speak at conferences or in classrooms. Still others have been referred to me by their professors or colleagues. In some cases, I'll meet them for twenty-five minutes for coffee. In others, we'll just have an email exchange in which they ask a few questions that I'll answer. The worst-case scenario (which happens more and more often these days) is that I won't have any time at all, but at least that person's name is now on my radar. Note: None of these are bad outcomes! If the people you reach out to can't meet with you, you're still in a better place than you were before reaching out. Regardless of the outcome, always thank the people who respond to you, email with you, or meet with you. Thank them immediately, specifically pointing to what you learned from them and how you'll apply that knowledge to your goals. Thank them profusely. And vow to pass on the favor someday to another up-and-coming podcaster when you're more established in your career.

- Take classes. I mentioned classes earlier in the feedback section. But podcasting classes give you far more than education and feedback. When you take classes, you also become a member of a community of other aspiring podcasters, and you give yourself a new podcasting mentor in the form of your instructor. Make the most of all these connections. Ask lots of questions in class, go out for drinks after class with your fellow students, and stay in touch with them and your instructor when the class ends. And don't worry about breaking the bank. Depending on where you enroll, classes can be expensive, inexpensive, or even free.

- Accept all invitations. Accept invitations from your fellow podcasting classmates and instructors to spend time together. Accept invitations to any networking event where podcasters may be present. If you're invited to join a new podcasting club in your area, join it. If you hear about a podcasting meet-up, attend it. And if you reach the point where you're being asked to sit on a panel or moderate one, always say yes.

Above all, embrace your identity as a podcaster. Have faith in yourself and your story. Know that the only requirement to call yourself a podcaster is to make podcasts. Make them, and then make some more. And then make them better and better. Make them as only you can.

You're a podcaster. I believe in you. And I'm so excited to hear what you put out into the world.

Final Thoughts: Yes You Can!

At this point, I'm hoping that most of you are ready to put down this book, grab your recording equipment, and go. If that's you, hooray! Embrace your voice! Share it with the world!

But for those of you who are still nervous, who are feeling overwhelmed, who are wondering if you really have it in you to make your podcast dreams come true, let me assure you: You do.

You have the basics right here in this book, but you also have something bigger: You have yourself, your life experiences, your perspective. And all those unique, horrible, beautiful things that make you who you are will help you tell the story you want in a way that only you can.

It doesn't matter if you're currently a part-time administrative assistant, a high school student, a retired firefighter. It doesn't matter if you've never picked up a microphone in your life. For the three decades before I was a podcaster, I also hadn't picked up a microphone (or edited audio or conducted an interview). For most of my life, the word "podcast" didn't even exist. But looking back, I was being trained my entire life to be podcaster. Let me explain.

You know how adults are always asking kids, "What do you want to be when you grow up?"

For me, my answer was almost always something related to writing or art. I liked drawing pictures and writing poetry and reading stories—but I didn't know exactly what I wanted to do for a living. Even after years of high school focused on literature and years of college focused on film studies (all while working at the entry-level full-time and part-time jobs to pay the bills), I didn't know.

My first job out of college was working for a nonprofit that taught classes and ran support groups over the phone. The students were, for the most part, housebound. Most were elderly. Some were living with disabilities. A number were living with AIDS.

I started out as an administrator, connecting students to classes, communicating with teachers, and writing copy for course catalogs. But within a few months I was also teaching.

Prior to this, I'd never taught. I'd been a nanny and a waitress. I'd been the person who picks up the phone when you call to complain about something you ordered in a catalog. I'd been a college journalist/administrative assistant/gas station attendant/hardware girl. In no uncertain terms: I wasn't a teacher.

But I realized that—in the unique environment in which I was teaching—my expertise meant little compared to my ability to make my students laugh, reminisce, and feel a little more connected to the world outside their apartments or nursing home bedrooms.

The nonprofit I worked for allowed me to create my own class on any topic I wanted. I chose film and television history—a subject that I'd studied extensively in college, and one that I've loved my whole life. Each week I'd visit a different decade in television and discuss what was happening in U.S. culture during that same time. The students had sharp memories for the shows we discussed and detailed stories about what their lives were like during those times.

The classes had no grades, and what the students learned was—frankly—not much. But I like to think that my classes fostered both a sense of community and empowerment. Sure, most of my students couldn't leave their homes, but all of them could turn on a television and look back on their own memories. And each week, whether we were discussing Lucy Ricardo or Archie Bunker, I tried to impart the message that consuming media was an act of participation—in history, in society's social debates, and in the consumer-driven machine that keeps America's economy going.

I enjoyed teaching my classes over the phone. But it wasn't really my lifelong dream—not that I knew what my dream was. I only knew that I loved storytelling, and I loved being connected to people and to history. Within a year and a half, I quit.

Little did I know that this first job would provide me with some of the most important skills for my life as a podcaster. And looking back, so did every job I'd ever held—from being the calm customer service representative people yelled at over the phone to being the administrative assistant who kept to a schedule. And I'm willing to bet that everything you've done up until now will also help you.

I'm speaking to all you stay-at-home parents who've mastered the art of boosting little people's spirits. I'm speaking to all you hardware girls (hooray, fellow hardware girls!) who have a knack for talking to strangers and making intimidating tools feel manageable. I'm talking to all of you who've never stepped foot in a radio studio or written a script or edited a single audio track.

You have it in you. Everything you've done up until now has prepared you for it. You've got this.

Acknowledgments

First and foremost, I want to thank everyone who encouraged me to write this book. More than a year before I ever sat down to type a single word, my friend and mentor Gretchen Rubin planted the idea in my head. With her trademark enthusiasm, she said, "You're the best person in the world to write it!"

My dear friend and co-host Jolenta Greenberg ran with the idea from there, insisting that I had it in me to do it. Then, putting her money where her mouth was, she introduced me to her agent, the outstanding Liz Parker.

Liz Parker has been nothing but enthusiastic and supportive from day one, helping me with my proposal, introducing my book to publishers, and making my dreams come true by landing me with the great people at William Morrow.

Thank you to my editor at William Morrow, the outstanding Cassie Jones, and to everyone else there, for helping me to make this book better while still staying true to my vision. The care, creativity, and enthusiasm they've all brought to the table have blown me away.

Huge thanks to my husband, Dean McRobie, who helped me put some of the technical aspects of podcast distribution into easy-to-understand English. And enormous thanks to podcaster extraordinaire Michele Siegel, who gave the whole thing a second set of eyes.

I also want to thank all my former colleagues at WNYC, who gave me the greatest boot camp in producing and hosting when I first started out. There are too many to name (I could list a hundred), but I must give a special thanks to Joel Meyer, who first brought me into the WNYC fold, and to Jim Colgan and Jay Cowit, who first sat down with me and taught me how to talk into a microphone and use the DAVID editing software. Thanks also to Ann Saini, who took an entire holiday weekend off to teach me how to use Hindenburg. And enormous thanks to Alex Johnson, who first said to me, "You sound just like you, and that's what makes you great."

Huge thanks to my beloved nonfiction team at Panoply: Laura Mayer, Mia Lobel, Sam Dingman, Ryan Dilley, Andrea Silenzi, Henry Molofsky, Chris Berube, Mary Wilson, Lindsey Kratochwill, Cameron Drews, Veralyn Williams, Jennifer Lai, Jayson DeLeon, Odelia Rubin, A. C. Valdez, Jacob Smith, Dan Bloom, Efim Shapiro, Ife Olujobi, Margaret Kelley, Jordan Bell, Hannah Cope, Ilana Millner, Samiah Adams, Christy Mirabal, Sarah Bentley, Bettina Warshaw, Carly Migliori, Jason Gambrell, Evan Viola, Lisa Fierstein, Nicole Buntsis, and Tina Tran. You've taught me not just how to be a better host but so much about the business of podcasting and the art of managing both projects and people.

And thank you to my new podcasting family at Stitcher, who swooped in when Panoply announced the end of their content arm—especially Chris Bannon, Kristin Myers, Nora Ritchie, Jared O'Connell, and Casey Holford.

I would be nothing without all the hugely talented co-hosts I've worked with. That includes Rafer Guzman (thank you so much for allowing me to be your co-host ten years ago, for constantly helping me improve, and for showing me how much fun it can be to talk with someone you like on mic), James Barr (I dream of a day when all people with your talent also have your level of kindness and professional-ism), and once again, Jolenta Greenberg (Jolenta, your humor, energy, and willingness to be vulnerable never fail to blow me away). I'm a better host and human because of all of you.

Huge thanks to all the media superheroes who saw me standing on the bottom rung of the ladder over the years, reached down, and hoisted me up: Kerry Donahue and Kerri Hoffman (and the merry band of superstar audio women they regularly assemble), Graham Griffith, June Thomas, Celeste Headlee, Hal Gessner, Caitlin Thompson, Ann Heppermann, and, again, the amazing Laura Mayer and Chris Bannon, are but a few.

Thanks also to every listener who's supported what I've done, written in with suggestions for how I can improve, and cheered for me along the way. I am eternally grateful to all of you.

Last but not least, thank you to my family and again to my dear husband, Dean. Dean, you're the best cheerleader in the world and the best explainer of difficult things. I love talking about my work with you, solving problems as a team, and knowing that you always have my back. Thank you, thank you.

Index